… Through Practices

Alex Arteaga
Heike Langsdorf
(eds.)

An Introduction to the Book Series

Choreography as Conditioning is a series of five books conceived and realized in the framework of the artistic research project *Distraction as Discipline*.[1] 'Choreography' is understood here, in a broad sense, as a way of organizing bodies in their surroundings, while 'conditioning' refers to the constraints introduced in a situation in order to become choreographic. The term 'choreography' also points to both the collective character of these processes *(choreo)* and to the generation of diverse kinds of signs *(graphy)*. 'Conditioning' implies the same semantic elements: collectivity *(con-)* and the production of, in this case, linguistic/oral signs *(ditioning* from *dicere,* to say).

Throughout the forty months in which *Distraction as Discipline* has been realized, and as one of its constitutive components, different groups of artist researchers were invited to write *through* their practices, that is, to develop practices of writing departing from the performance of collective artistic/aesthetic research practices in different media. Accordingly, each book in this series addresses different thematic fields on the basis of the intertwined performance of different research practices in different constellations and presents some of the resulting artifacts: a collection of texts.

The ground on which this book series emerges is thus an open-ended, dynamic network of relational practices. The books contribute to this network by fostering an observational attitude

1. Distraction as Discipline – An investigation into the function of attention and participation in performance art and art pedagogy / Langsdorf & Luyten 2016 – 2019.

in the processes of writing and reading. Instead of being a conclusion of the dynamics that lead to their generation, these books aim to keep these dynamics alive and vague enough in order to enable variable insights, open trajectories of sense, and further forms of inquiry. This requires spaces and times for reenacting, revisiting, requestioning, and therefore avoiding non-critical consolidations of preconfigured systems of ideas. In this sense, this book series intends to create conditions for addressing, among many others, the following question: How, where, and by whom do things get organized and what kinds of spheres of experience are made im/possible by the practices we perform and encounter?

Alex Arteaga & Heike Langsdorf

An Introduction to the Fifth Book

...*Through Practices*—the last book of the series Choreography as Conditioning—is a collection of resonances, written by researchers involved in the realization of the three-day public symposium with the same title. This gathering invited artist researchers to explore ecologies of attention, awareness, and the sense of participation. A variety of guided and hosted artistic/aesthetic/somatic research practices operated as a medium for this open-ended exploration into the agencies of practices within these ecologies.

The conception of the symposium departed from a differentiation between those who offer a practice and those dedicated to witness the development of the resulting processes. The symposium's setting—a constellation of practices and the intertwinement of intentions and foci of inquiry—contributed definitively to blurring this differentiation. Everyone ran and/or participated in specific practices and practiced witnessing. Observation, therefore, practiced in different ways, became a common ground for ...*Through Practices*.

This symposium was the last event of the research project *Distraction as Discipline* at KASK. As such, it was a further manifestation of Heike Langsdorf's interest in reclaiming attention and participation as a resistant potential in art and art pedagogy in times of massive digital technification. The main strategy throughout this research project has been to present organizational, spatial, social, and communicational sets of conditions that allow people to become part of something that happens *with* them instead of *to* or *for* them—frames of collective and individual empowerment through the recognition and performance of individual and collective agencies.

In this sense, the conception and design of *...Through Practices* was as important as the performance of each practice, the gathering of reflections, and the flow of thoughts that continue after the three days of the symposium. It made sense, thus, to ask all the researchers concerned with shaping the symposium including ourselves to 'write though their practices' and contribute to the collection of texts—the artifacts produced through our writing processes—that you are holding in your hands. Consequently, this book presents sedimentations resulting from different ways of approaching individual, shared and collective practices. They mirror different forms of participating and responding—different in/capacities, im/possibilities, and dis/interests related to the specificities of what each of us experienced. How do we perceive to be invited? How do we react to openness, vagueness, and given structures and rules? How do we interact with more or less explicit ideologies, desires, necessities, traumas, obsessions, missions,...?

These and related questions critically condition the intertwined logics (the ecologies) of our attention, awareness, curiosity, and engagement. In the liminal spaces that the systemic organization of all these relationships enable, our interests—our being *(-esse,* to be) in between *(inter-)*—change. Their variations can be seen in the texts of this book and now, with perspective, in the texts of the book series that here comes to an end. In the path that all these texts pave can be seen, not only how our being-in-between (our interests) but also how the directions towards we extend them (our intentions), what hold us together (our contents), and what allows us to be in touch (our contingencies) are conditioned through practices.

We would like to thank the authors of the following texts not only for their contributions to the book but also for having made ... *Through Practices* possible.

Alex Arteaga & Heike Langsdorf

you're less
*researching the
practice of witnessing*

Julien Bruneau

After some time spent discussing
The life and death of a rooster
The how and the law around turning
—or rather not?—the feathery
Infuriated being into a meal,
One acknowledges one's hands
Persistently covered in red
And takes the look of naked beetroots
Peeled and sunk in water
Eleven dense little hearts
Weighing, waiting, tainting.

After some time spent in the wordless handling
Of vegetables, cleansing and chopping,
All drawn into the muteness of the craft
And infused with burned scent,
One sits inside, plunged into
A milieu of curated awareness where
Vectors of attention get lobbed
Above circles of speech and then
Bounce onto screens, expand through windows,
Slip into the move of sparse music notes
A caring turntablist makes whirl around.

After some time spent in witnessing,
Time itself is to be attended to,
Inhabited, met and cheered:
Here it is! With its currents, its rhythms
Shaping then dismantling groups
Enlivening then draining people
Making sun spots travel
Turning down the day
Loosening the mind and the mouths
Who, now, throw themselves
Into a last embrace of speech
Savoring the erotic of problematics
That fuels the dedication to questions.

Some say
—driven by the lust of participation,
Enmeshment, horizontality and care—
Some say
That witnessing is *with*-nessing,
It is to actively take part,
Immersed, at no remove,
Engaged in the plurality
Of things and events and beings
Embracing the anarchic mess at the heart of it all
As that from which, indeed, wit may rise and glow
—witnessing as wit-*messing*—

But, when a witness,
Dear to my heart is also
The distance that nurtures
The recess that dances
The spaciousness that blooms
The open field that shines.
If witnessing is *with*-nessing
It is also, I say, *without*-nessing
The process, that is,
by which *-nesses* get dropped,
Qualities, conditions and states suspended.
'Témoin' is what Frenchs say
Witness is, yes, 'témoin'
't'es moins' is also what French hear
'T'es moins' is, yes, 'you're less'
'Cause to be witness
Is to be less
Is to lessen your you
So you listen
Don't you?

———

On a large white wall
Beamed light cuts away
Dense clusters of darkness,
Tiny figures that propagate swiftly,
Popping out from heard waves of keystrokes.

On the smooth concrete floor
Loops of wires run through large
Dotted and mineral curves,
Words painstakingly drawn one day ago,
Dot by dot made of stones
That brought with them
—testimonies of their biotope—
Rubbish, dust, moss and whatnots.

While in the air
A voice circulates
That rewires in its listeners
The apparatus of perception
Taste to ears
Sound to nostrils
Sight to skin,
One is sitting
Face to face
With the rift
At the core
Of one's notebook
Open on one's lap
To which point, is it written,
Is the practice of witnessing
Amounting to the practice
Of deciphering in the maze
Sketched by my labile awareness
The words that will bear testimony
To my attentive attentional dedication?

In the third verse, the phrase "erotic of problematics" is borrowed
   from Anna Luyten who used it in a reporting session during
   the symposium.

MIXING

From the silence of an empty space to the fullness of
activities overlapping, there is always sound. Things
change while you are listening and listening again.
Transforming the space by feeding back, stomaching
and cooking the many voices, as in eating and sleeping.
Resonance can be writing, writing can be resonance.

> Short description of Fransien van der Putt's practice as it appeared
> in the ...*Through Practices* program.

On (not) mixing different spaces and dancing with micro-events

Fransien van der Putt

01. THIS IS NOT AN EXHIBITION

Writing about my participation in ...*Through Practices* in times of corona is not easy. Coming together 'through practices,' as Heike Langsdorf proposed once more during the last days of October 2019 at KASK in Ghent, seems like the ultimate way of responding to matters of crisis and radical change: to share time and space while attending to how things are going, without already pretending to know what to do or how to act; to postpone (or "distract ourselves from," as Heike would call it) what the swift solutions proposed by apps, other tech, and more general modes of a so-called efficiency society and industry. Could we allow for a slower, less goal-oriented approach, "to explore the ecology of one's personal attention and sense for participation"? Unfortunately, this kind of coming together is hardly possible at the moment.

NON-LINEAR

When inviting me to join this "co-designing process," Heike Langsdorf had never listened to my text mixes or soundscapes. We had enjoyed quite a few conversations and she must have read one or two of my articles, but those gave little clues about the work I did as a mixer of texts at Radio 100, from the late eighties until the early two thousands, in Amsterdam.

My text mixes are rough, since they don't exhibit the linear logic of speech and reading, while never really reaching a kind of musical transcendence either. For me, the voices reflect the many manners of the world. By being layered on top of each other, they disclose other features or qualities than they were intended to have. The mixes could be considered as conversations, but they are definitely not. The entanglement of voices from different contexts and social positions produce a strange, poetic matter, moving away from the obvious in social regimes and common behavior.

One could compare the text mixes to having many guests at a table, or to being in a choir, a busy bar, a marketplace, or a shopping mall. But those gatherings, also confusing and fascinating in the way voices mix as people act out, still share a common space. With this I don't only mean the real space of the situation, but rather the imagined spaces people refer to in conversation, which are equally governed by regimes. French psychoanalist Jacques Lacan called this "dominant discourse" and French philosopher Louis Althusser described its logic as "the function of interpellation," when he pointed to the effect of regimes on our behavior: how ideas get into our head and have an effect on our lives to such an extent that we believe them to be our own.

DIFFERENT SPACES

The mechanics of mixing records, recorded audio, and life feed from the mic, the telephone in the studio, online connections and files *(Radio 100* was the first in Holland to stream online) allows for a layering or mixing of different spaces, not common to each other, not dominated by one specific set of regimes.

The layering creates uncommon distances and intimacies, ranging from social realms to artistic domains. Existing inside each other, by being mixed together, they merge and contrast at the same time. The mix produces abstraction and concreteness, talks about something particular and at the same time about many things, and often ends up being close to (but never quite) just noise. A myriad of places is addressed and, since destinies vary by the swift arrival and departure of a great diversity of sources, slowly weave together as much as they fall apart. There is no stable, common, or given object to display.

Questions of grammar and syntax, of genres and subgenres, manners of speaking and phrasing, the different languages and their *official* pronunciations or accents and dialects, voices singing or reading, language being consciously acted out or accidentally uttered and recorded: it doesn't really matter who is speaking, but more that these singular voices start to dance around with each other and form strangely new or different, scrambled sentences. Contexts are broken open and, therefore, emphasized and questioned. When deconstructing and reassembling, you can feel dominant discourse seeking affirmation, as much as you start to realize where the cracks are.

    Inspired by the Dutch composer and theatre artist Dick Raaijmakers in his book *De Methode:* "dit bij dat en toen" [this with that and then], form and content are ripped apart to form not so much new meaning but to work the sediments of culture, putting the destination of utterances and statements into question, when listening to what is left and cannot be denied, after the storm of mixing, cutting apart, and repeating had done its job.

TRUST

Heike's invitation to join ... *Through Practices* radiated a strange form of trust in me. Regarding the many participating voices, I could see the relation between her proposal for a constellation of practitioners and practices and my mixing. It was all about letting people, in their own tempo and from their own perspective, realize things together, without having to experience the same thing or to agree on, or even understand, every step. Artistic production would go beyond the obligatory modern 'new' and the postmodern 'broken.' Proposals would result from mindful, open, and inclusive group negotiations using intuitive means and slow building techniques—not yet knowing, risking failure, finding out, learning by doing.

    Meaning could not be produced for others, could not be produced yet, but would be composed together in time, as a form of emergence, by being affected by each other, leaving space for others as much as finding some for oneself—not by deciding on how to apply the rules or steer for a certain outcome, but by finding out in process.

Through parallel practices, a liminal space or experience would be emphasized, not only between, but also inside practices, as they were rubbing against or crossing each other in the shared space. The whole event seemed to be a common writing exercise with bodies, space, time, and scores addressing and being addressed by each body involved.

ATTENTION

It may seem obvious to mention one wants to organize attention with art, dance, or choreography, but I understood right away that the importance of ...*Through Practices* lay in the undoing or working away from certain dichotomies, like doing and thinking, or performing and witnessing.

For my fellow practitioners during ...*Through Practices,* it seemed rather important to emphasize the real or actual time and space needed for this kind of attention. It was as if they were trying to counter the speed of 'hyperficial' communion and communication delivered by our common tech devices and the current societal regime, which allow us no time to develop our own voice within, or as, the common.

Actually, my practice of mixing records, recordings, and live streams of speech doesn't align very much with this desire to slow down and dismantle the logic of short attention span and quick results. In the late 1980s, when I started doing my mixing, a punk, dada, or avantgarde approach fueled by disruption and rather violent provocation was still very welcome. Risk was normal, and destruction was still a typical battleground in relation to institutional power regimes. Of course, minimal and ambient forms of music and dance had challenged this, but not to the extent that has been recognized today.

NO SCORE

Only when participating at the event at Zwarte Zaal/ KASK did I realize that many of the proposed scores had similarities to my practice as a mixer—if not in protocol, then certainly in the form the practices produced. Things would unfold slowly, in due time, allowing for the different layers of a practice to unveil themselves to the participants. Through a broken linearity and experimental forms of paralleling, disrupting, or restructuring the linear logic of purpose and resolution, the practices would arrive at unexpected, even wild moments through accumulation, as the outcome of an open composition, sometimes connected to failure or a transgressive relation to the rules of the score. Endings would often occur by arriving at some kind of standstill or silence, as new, but different beginnings of a phased and infinite process.

SILENCE

During the event of ... *Through Practices,* I also came to realize that the silence that now started to govern the room, as a unspoken agreement between the many practitioners, was allowing little space for my audiophonic interferences. I was assigned an end of the day slot of 15 minutes, imagined as a burst of sound and feedback. While participating in other people's practices during the first day and thinking about what to do in the end, I realized that I didn't want to do that conclusion. So, I went back to old fashioned mixing, starting after the first break on Monday. Against the protocol, one could say.

WILD CARD

During preparations, I never really worried about not having a score. From the beginning of my involvement, I relied on the in between of liminal perception and micro-modulations that the cohabitation or constellation of practices would produce. What I didn't realize was that my practice was rather traditional, in the sense that I was just 'sending,' and not inviting anyone explicitly into my practice.

A wild card is a card that can take on any value in the game and doesn't have to qualify before entering. It is also described as causing uncertainty because of the unpredictability of its behavior. Being caught up in the midst of these various co-existing practices—experiencing, relating, connecting, and reflecting on them one after the other or in a parallel, overlapping manner—and trying to find a space or make room for other voices, I was more and more questioning what my mix actually could add. Wasn't the idea to not change the situation in the room too much, in order for things to emerge?

NO FEEDBACK

I had decided beforehand that I was not going to do traditional feedback, as in recording sound in the room (people's breath, sensitive intercourse, or discussions) and feeding it back. As a form, feedback is very aesthetic, but it also confirms and emphasizes what is already going on. If anything should be added to the space in terms of sound and voices, it should open up the space (and not over-establish it by exhibiting or objectifying the things that were already there).

So I decided to add voices that would be alien timbres and tempi recalibrating the room, as a kind of off-circuit making space for 'others' to come in and making people feel welcome without having to align or engage— to extend the space by inserting other spaces.

RESPECT

So, what to think of and how to deal with this general, unwritten rule governing ... *Through Practices* (that of respect through silence in the room)? At a certain point, the silence establishing itself in the room felt monumental, and almost intimidating to people (surely those who were just arriving). Did the openness and the decentralizing of purpose or goal lead to more and more silence? Was there a kind of control or discipline entering the room through silence? And even if this were the case, how would I relate to this? Would breaking it open help visitors to enter, or would it make their transition into a collective process even more difficult by filling the necessary gaps they had to cross in order to find their own perceptual relation, their own sense of agency within the constellation of practices, co-writing, or co-designing?

My sound system could rip open the constellation of silences and concentration with the slightest push of one button. How could my mixing add to, interfere with, or even just highlight or foreground the actual listening in the room? How could my mix relate to the in-between-spaces, add to a liminal or decentralized perception, foster a feeling of diversity in open scores, and make everybody's sensory faculties of listening, witnessing, or acting out equal? Would my wild card, my liminal hosting work, beyond distracting and disturbing others in the room, find a function or a role to play?

> 02. ... *THROUGH PRACTICES,* COMING BACK TO THE UNFULFILLED (Can we please do this again?)

The practices proposed were meant to open up habit and transform the act of checking in on fulfillment of expectation into something else. How could I facilitate that trajectory and create a general sense of curiosity, exploration, and trust (opposite to obligation and purpose) by providing an atmosphere that was light, but still serious enough for everyone and everything to proceed?

COHABITATION

Working the same room with different practices could be regarded as a form of cohabitation. In French politics, this refers to a president being elected from another (opposite) political inclination than the existing government. Having two masters in the house comes with a logic of position and transgression. ... *Through Practices* speculated on a different logic—one of working the same space with different, but not necessarily opposing, actors. The constellation of artistic researchers aligned artists and their guests (implicated or random spectators becoming both witnesses and participants) not in terms of this or that ideological affiliation, but in terms of a variety of activities that generated specific forms of attention, mostly through an enhanced bodily engagement, with diverse resulting modes of reflection.

WELLNESS

When mixing in voices—as such or in songs—and other sounds, I hesitated, since I knew how much even the smallest sound would influence people's perception, consciously and unconsciously. Sound travels in all directions and has a direct appeal to the body. Laura Oriol, who was invited as a documenting participant, wondered during the feedback session on the last day whether ... *Through Practices* allowed for tension or resistance. She was confronted with a sense of shame around her own dissent. Oriol said: "I don't want to conform to the wellness." Were my soft interferences only adding to the wellness or did they function as interpellation to re-establish the existing order of silence and respect? Did I manage to dance around with the micro-events in the room and make them grow into a subtle form of dissent?

FEEDING BACK AND FORTH

Thinking about the logic of feeding back and forth
in the room and the ambiguous territory suggested
by ... *Through Practices,* I reread Brian Massumi's
introduction to his book *Parables for the Virtual* (2002),
in which he points to the importance of paying attention
to how the body and change are connected through
movement and sensation. He notes how critical theory
failed to pay attention to what the specificities of moving
and feeling do for the body and change.

Massumi qualifies processes of signification
as "feedback" and "feedforward." He assumes that the
stability of position or meaning comes after. "Position
no longer comes first, with movement a problematic
second. [Position] is secondary to movement, and
derived from it. It is retro movement, movement residue.
The problem is no longer how there can be change
given positioning. The problem is to explain the wonder
that there can be stasis given the primacy of process."[1]
Massumi argues that movement and sensation,
or feeling, are processes in time; they are actually the
first things to happen or arrive, and only in retrospect
meaning and truth are produced, "as feedback."
And, complicating this, these forward and backward
movements happen at the same time.

I read Massumi's argument as an attempt to
transcend the stultification that comes with thinking and
acting out dichotomies, from understanding process as
linear and defined by position and transgression instead
of emergence. It is in this micro-attention to the folding
qualities of events that we can 'feel' reality altering and
being shaped in the first place.

1. Brian Massumi, Parables for the Virtual. Movement, Affect,
Sensation (Durham & London: Duke University Press,
2002), 7-8.

FOLDS, POCKETS AND ENVELOPES

My main concern during ... *Through Practices* was how to not close the space, allow for some unwarranted or unforeseen movement back and forth, without it becoming transgressive, extra, or alien. Letting a certain wildness in to open up the silence, without destroying the necessary concentration and focus. How could my mixing open up the space, make people walk further, act freer, allow for things to emerge, for disturbance and distraction to become part of the deal?

    I guess one answer emerged while I was trying to disappear in the context of the other practices. I was looking for folds, for pockets and envelopes in the room. I started to add 'natural' mini-movements—like a breeze, a flock of birds, or an insect passing. I hacked the other practices on a liminal level, by entering their pockets, leaving little envelopes under their door, without any form of demonstrative looping or backfeeding, trying to not add a new work or another practice to the floor. Which sounds like a contradiction, but maybe it is not.

    I guess I tried to enhance and overwrite by playing with the slight repositioning of things (both in time and space), adding a durational aspect through dysfunctional repetition, and foregrounding and backgrounding things with a variety of sound materials and volumes dispersed in the room. I let forms of noise enter the room and tried to find a place for them—not so much to regenerate the unnatural silence in an expo-room (one could just open the window for that), but to keep the 'scape of things' moving forward, through upstaging a few small 'aliens.' Maybe it made the space less formal, less predictable, and more chaotic, like the relative silence one finds in, for instance, a public garden.

26

Time and time again

Emilie Gallier

what has been left out during the genesis
what has been covered
what dissolves

poetic documentation practice
a score for groups
protocol

COLLECTING

The gathering:

selection

ongoing
precaire presence
mon & wed 1
all days   every day

TIME

Imagine an encounter

Cut, cut, cut. Cæsuras that set the frame for relations to occur,

Doors are

not allowed

from where we

READ

heterotopia

for more 'togetherness' we need to be together

AND

Re

ritual

believe that the information of those who came
before us is somehow inside us.

ATTENTION AND PARTICIPATION

attending the moment "some or some"

Practice. Practice. Repeat.

Real

seems to dissolve whereas details grow more and more
important.

gray jacket

caterpillar

Practice
Practice
Repeat

contemplation.

Dominik's jacket is

two yellow

I SPEAK   I AGREE

All rituals

TIME

AGAIN

Time and time again is a collage inspired by the practices presented at the 2019 symposium ... *Through Practices*. I witnessed *The dance of the day* by Heike Langsdorf on October 28. I engaged with *THE WAVE* by Anouk Llaurens for the entire duration of this symposium (three days). I participated in *From where we are* by Miriam Rohde and Laetitia Gendre on October 29, I cooked with Bilal Kamilla Arnout and with other participants. One of my main strategies in creating these pages is reiteration. In waves, like in breath, reiteration is a repetitive gesture that I experience as a characteristic of the practices of art and research in ... *Through Practices*. In the spirit of reiteration, the collage looks back and borrows from the three former books in the series *Choreography as Conditioning*. From the first book *Thinking Conditioning through Practice* (Arteaga, Langsdorf 2018) I literally cut and paste words by Julien Bruneau (p.34, p.36), Laetitia Gendre and Miriam Rohde (p.19), and Heike Langsdorf (p.89). From the second book (Andersen, Langsdorf 2019) I take words by Barbara Raes (p.50, p.51, p.53), Boyzie Cekwana (p.19), and Heike Langsdorf (p.22). From the third book *The Orphans of Tar* (de Smet et. al 2019) I cut words that were assembled by Julien de Smet, Ronny Heiremans, Heike Langsdorf, Vanessa Müller, Filip Van Dingenen, Stijn Van Dorpe, Clémentine Vaultier, and Katleen Vermeir (p.34, p.36, p.40).

Time and time again is imbued with the presence of water. This is inspired by *THE WAVE* by Anouk Llaurens, and by *In waves,* the graphic novel by Aj Dungo (2019). Water is present in these pages through the wave-like composition, the process of dissolution of paper in a cup of water, and the confluences of practices. In the background of these practical manifestations, water is also present in these pages as a trope, where attention is proposed as a valuable resource to be protected and cared for, like clean water (Crawford 2015).

References

Andersen, Tawny and Heike Langsdorf eds., Practicing Futures through Voicing. Ghent: Art Paper Editions, 2019.
Arteaga, Alex and Heike Langsdorf eds., Thinking Conditioning through Practice. Ghent: Art Paper Editions, 2018.
Crawford, Matthew B.. "The Cost of Paying Attention." The New York Times, 2015. Accessed March 2 2020. https://www.nytimes.com/2015/03/08/opinion/sunday/the-cost-of-paying-attention.html>.
De Smet, Julien et. al. The Orphans of Tar – A Speculative Opera. Ghent: Art Paper Editions, 2019.
Dungo, Aj. In Waves. London: Casterman, 2019.

FRAGILE COMMUNITY S/CORE

The *Fragile Community S/Core* is a tool for exploring the concept of temporary community through collective doing/thinking. It proposes a system of interactions where varied aesthetic experiences can coexist, challenge and inspire each other. This is done by formulating a series of questions and responses coming from the artistic practices of the participants and the context in which they take place. The score is a process oriented study based on a set of instructions for co-practicing and documenting.

Short description of Lilia Mestre's practice as it appeared in the
... Through Practices program.

Fragile Community S/Core. A *Scorescapes* iteration for ...*Through Practices*

Lilia Mestre

Scorescapes. Thinking scores as a pedagogical tool is an ongoing research framework developed by performing artist and researcher Lilia Mestre at a.pass (advanced performance and scenography studies), an educational platform for artistic research based in Brussels. *Scorescapes* are realized through formulating a series of questions and responses coming from the artistic practice of the participants. *Scorescapes* consists of a set of instructions (a score) for practicing and documenting collective processes that can be used and adapted by whoever is interested in the practice.

For the symposium ... *Through Practices,* a new *Scorescapes* iteration, *Fragile Community S/Core,* was conceived as an instrument for building a temporary collective through conducting artistic research in a semi-public environment. The score proposed a system of interactions where varied aesthetics, tools, concepts, and forms could coexist, complement, challenge, and inspire each other.

Fragile Community S/Core (see the score below) sought to underline the importance of the experiential aspect of learning together as thinking partners and as active community makers in co-composition. The importance of the collective was emphasized by ... *Through Practices'* semi-public context. The participants of the score simultaneously shared their individual practices with the *Fragile Community S/Core* group and probed how these practices interacted in this specific environment. This situation raised questions of inclusion, trust, participation, focus, and spectatorship in an active manner.

The presence of the 'dedicated witnesses,' who observed the unfolding of the practice and engaged in the resulting feedback discussions, was very important in the general process. They made clear the role of the viewer (audience) as an active presence and constitutive element of the process of sharing. Furthermore, they also contributed to the reflection about knowledge exchange and co-learning environments. They made clear, although not necessarily explicit, this central question: What is the response-ability of the viewer?

Fragile Community S/Core was the first *Scorescapes* iteration realized in a semi-public framework. *Scorescapes* are designed to be practiced in an atelier situation with a predetermined group of people. Everyone performs and is, at the same time, the audience. *Scorescapes* is conceived as a private practice with a high level of concentration. It was a great experience to expand the spectrum of participation with a non-informed audience and to find bridges to develop the practice in vulnerable environments, just as it was to understand and discuss which conditions enable certain ways of doing.

One of the fundamental and most relevant aspects of ... *Through Practices* was to attempt to make artistic research practices public. In my understanding, making the process an accomplice of the research, and thinking about modes of sharing, gives visibility to the complex assemblages of references and partnerships that research carries. These are critical aspects to consider in order to create infrastructures that sustain knowledge processes and production.

In this sense, the gesture of asking the *Fragile Community S/Core* participants to bring their practices in a backpack refers (as per the score below) to the idea that artistic research (and art practice) are analogic to life: it embeds people histories, social class, gender, economies... as much as they are in correlation to the 'traveler artist,' who is always on the move and always dependent on institutional infrastructures. The artist or artist researcher is in constant displacement between contexts as a form of learning and creating. What are the consequences of this state?

The practices of arriving, questioning, observing, trying, reflecting, accessing, exchanging, and showing

in specific contexts call for a situated awareness of
the tools of the researcher(s) and the conditions that
enable the work to be done. What, why, how, and where
do things take place? With whom? Bringing these
aspects to the fore as resources for artistic research
problematizes learning environments, from the school
to the theatre (or similar environments of gathering
and exposure), and their implications on modes of
production and distribution of art and artistic research.

In another sense, the backpack also makes
reference to the resilience, and thus, implicitly, to the
precarity of the artist or artist researcher always already
ready to take opportunities for development and to
form fragile and temporary collectives.

FRAGILE COMMUNITY S/CORE

Bring your practice in a backpack. We will
arrive at ... *Through Practices* as visitors.
We will unpack our backpacks each time we
meet and pack them up again at the end of
each session.

We will be there where everyone is.
We will practice in between other practices.

We will observe while we practice. We will
be observed. We will write and we will talk
between other unpredictable movements.

We can shift spaces to find where it is better
to be. We will sense and choose the limits of
our space.

Once we are settled, everyone will prepare
an individual five minute presentation of
their practice.

We will determine by chance who will ask a question to whom before starting the presentations.

Everyone will present her/his/their five minutes.

After all the presentations, we will set a timeframe in which to individually formulate a question to another participant (half hour for example).

We will read the questions out loud and discuss them.

We will set a time to work individually on the responses (one hour for example).

We will restart a new cycle by presenting the responses again in a five minute time frame.

We determine by chance who will ask a question to whom before starting the presentations.

After this moment, the score will be settled and will develop spontaneously.

We will have three sessions of three hours and one session of four hours together.

I want to thank the participants of *Fragile Community S/Core* in the framework of ... *Through Practices:* Jaco Sette, Delphine Mertens, May Abnet, Loeke Vanhoutteghem and Alexandra Jacxsens.

NERVOUS SYSTEMS

Practicing *Nervous Systems* … encircles cracks between experiencing and understanding dance and choreography … tests environments where the body is not in search for any ideal centeredness … exercises becoming aware of forgetting, losing attention, and misunderstanding … almost always starts with extending awareness and vision … is somatic practicing disguised as a social experiment … drives on the experiences that are already in play and their resonance.

Short description of Klaas Devos' practice as it appeared in the
… *Through Practices* program.

Dance research in spite of Nervous Systems

Klaas Devos

In October 2019, I had the opportunity to present my artistic research practice for three consecutive days at the event ...Through Practices. The structure of this gathering was to witness and actively explore ten such practices. In this text, I will articulate the notion of dancing as research by introducing my practice and by revisiting its sessions during this event.

Somatic dance practices are held together by their intriguing inquiry of movement through the experience of expanding awareness of sensations. Such an experiential perspective is based on the principle that sensations are ways of penetrating and gaining insights into activities. I became familiar with this approach to dance during my conservatory training in classical, modern, and contemporary dance studies. There, I trained in Body-Mind Centering (BMC), which is an improvisation-based somatic practice that focuses on expanding awareness in order to increase one's movement vocabulary and choreographic possibilities. In general, somatic practices taught me that virtuosity is not only a matter of control and form, and that dance improvisations are based on our consciousness and awareness of decision-making rather than on achieving creative results.

  A BMC-session starts with a host introducing physiological issues and body systems, for example the respiratory system, the skeletal system, etc. In the first constellation of the practice, the participants listen to the host while comfortably lying down on the floor with their eyes closed, and sometimes supported by a practice partner's touch. The practitioners are considered 'active receivers,' a name that refers to their relaxed engagement, induced by a prosaic voice guiding their visualizations. Gradually, the host instructs them to explore the body systems in an introspective dance:

an improvised solo composition of sensing in motion. During the closure of the practice, these dances are revisited. Everyone is invited into a circle to recollect the dance and its sensations; in a personal narrative, the participants share their experiences with the group, allowing dialogue, associations, and differences to surface.

Differing from the traditional function of somatic practices as therapeutic practices, I apply extending awareness as an artistic and aesthetic dance research.[1] In my artistic research practice, I use the previously introduced structure of BMC, specify its physiological issues, and adapt the exercises in order to investigate and experiment with the moment of interpretation in improvised dance and instant choreography. I reframe BMC as an artistic and aesthetic dance research which I named *Nervous Systems*. It is a practice that strives to gain knowledge on dance by integrating notions from experimental phenomenology and neuro- and cognitive sciences.

---

1. It helps me to make a distinction between the artistic and aesthetic properties of dance as research practice. My artistic research deals with properties that are concerned with the construction and techniques of dance practice. For example, I investigate how different organizations and formulations of movement instructions make my improvisation practice more or less comprehensive for the practitioners. These artistic properties are precise, manageable, and can be named or defined in research. When I research aesthetic properties of dance, my perspective shifts from construction and techniques to appearances and experiences of sensations. Aesthetic research makes me approach my practice more intuitively and with more sensitivity to what emerges from the flow of the dance, of the experience of dancing itself. For example, I investigate how one dance affects me or others; I research when its play with appearances and disappearances makes us conscious, captivates us, or disrupts our being with it, as a dancer, researcher, or spectator. In other words, artistic and aesthetic properties of dance are intertwined, but they are not interchangeable components of my research practices.

When I practice *Nervous Systems,* I consider dance in a defined time and space; I understand this spatiotemporal framework as a habitat that functions as a safer place in which to experiment with physical sensations and imaginations. In contrast to the open character of my artistic and aesthetic dance research, this habitat is a finite place and time. The moving and attention of the participants needs to be confined in order to experiment with actions and activities, in order to grasp these and fictionalize them, and eventually to interpret these as movement or choreographic materials. In *Nervous Systems,* this territory for experimentation is marked with tape, chalk, light, etc. and limited in time by a clock, timekeeper, or soundtrack. These elements mark off a safer place, a place where normative or everyday relations to time, space, and embodiment do not limit the practice. To consider the spatiotemporal framework in which the aesthetic experiment of *Nervous Systems* takes place is a necessary agreement among participants that helps them to fully explore dance as actions in a non-judgmental way.

Nervous Systems opens up a hybrid study between science and dance. More precisely, it inquires into how anatomy and neuro- and cognitive sciences can be implemented as a technique for researching dance improvisation aesthetics. It investigates bodily centeredness and other idealizations of embodiment through dancing. As a derivative of somatic practices, it mobilizes expanding awareness in order to localize a different range of movements of the body in dance, a range that encompasses more than anatomy and kinesiology. It is by loosening the tight rope between dance and corporeality that *Nervous Systems* explore the possibilities of different forms of cognitive states in dance, thereby broadening our understanding of what repercussions concepts such as centeredness, balance, and control have on embodiment in dance improvisation.

At ... *Through Practices,* I limited the explicit contextualization of *Nervous Systems* to a minimum. Almost immediately, I asked participants to find a comfortable place close to the ground and started narrating a visualization that made them familiar with the research systems: the central and peripheral nervous system and the sensorial apparatus. The practice was introduced by taking as a reference my personal studio routine.[2] Every day of ... *Through Practices,* I changed the experiments in relation to the shared space, the time of the day, and the expectations of the participants. The first day, I presented the score for the improvisation in four short sentences; the second day, I made the group wait in a demarcated space before presenting them the score; on the last day, I repeated the structure of the practice of day one and asked the group to enter, exit, and re-enter the space 'anew,' before starting.[3] I rely on these elusive activities—that is, the unclear performativity of waiting and not dancing—in order to extend awareness in the practice and stimulate participants to start experimenting together. The setting of *Nervous Systems* is a fragile frame that grounds the little discomfort of experimenting and consequently generates a tension between our understanding and our performing of the score. The practice focuses awareness on this tension, and explores it as a place and time that allows the emergence of dance aesthetics.

During these experiments, I encourage the group to hold on to their feelings and to find nuances in what is happening in and around them. I try to help them by sharing my personal associations and by acknowledging

---

2. My studio routine: I lie down, listen to a self-prerecorded visualization, make breathing exercises, after about half an hour I get impatient and begin improvising while the last part of the recording turns into background noises.
3. The score reads: "In silence and shoulder blades cannot touch the floor: 1) Perform waiting, 2) explore noticing and awareness, 3) do nothing, not dancing, 4) resurface, 5) relate and flirt."

how the themes of the visualization resonate in the emerging dance composition. However, I have to refrain myself from explaining what we are doing and instead make them trust their own agencies by performing the score. This figuring out of the score and the searching for the boundaries of the improvisation causes a puzzling feeling of uncertainty, doubt, and unease—all sensations that might precede curiosity and awareness. The empty rhythms of these 'non-activities' destabilize traditional notions of being active and passive, participating and witnessing, dancing and not dancing.

In short, this seemingly aimless experiment is confusing; it destabilizes how we experience time, space, and movements. The basic strategy of *Nervous Systems* consists of a suspending dynamic. It aims to bring performers together to anticipate improvisation and allows them to wait and clarify what is happening with their relation to dance and choreographic aesthetics.

At this destabilizing stage in the practice, the group dynamic gains momentum. Participants are at a tilting point in developing the tasks or states that make up the score. Heads are turning to find support in the gaze of co-participants; this mental reassurance supports the group to take agency in this ambiguous dance. The tasks 'perform waiting,' 'explore noticing and awareness,' and 'do nothing/not dancing' stretch their horizon of attention, and the participants recognize structures in what seems to be random, group constellations and causalities. These recognitions are compasses to let a favorable direction and a plausible path of decision-making emerge in their unfolding improvisation. Through small digressions of their alertness, the participants 'resurface,' intervene, and temporarily dissolve the growing suspense. The dance is still minimal: small adjustments, some walking material, and twitching fingers. Similar to the visualization exercise, participants gently take control, either by improvising a playful way to deal with their unease, or by interrupting the tranquility and slow continuity in an anxious or nervous physical outburst. The score directs the participants to 'flirt and relate' with this sense of control; this translates into their nervous systems by experimenting with the impact of impulses on the sensitive web that is spun between their physical sensations, imaginations, and the real time and space.

During ... *Through Practices,* I integrated a group reflection to close my practice. Similar to BMC, I asked the participants to gather in a circle and exchange their experiences and thoughts in first-person narratives. In these monologues, they describe their dances; their words circulate around what they recalled of the improvisation, creating a selection of moments translated into words. As such, some participants contributed to a rather fragmented and incomplete image, a multi-perspective narrated reconstruction of the dance experiment. I'm skeptical about the critical function of this reporting activity, and I wonder how it contributes to the dancing as research in *Nervous Systems*. I sense that these words not only miss, but also lack the power to grasp, the tacit nature of our dancing. In order to transform improvised dance into a reliable source of information, the storytelling generates a montage of passed sensations. Verbal languages filter, tranquillize, or excite experiences, which results in (mis)representations. These verbal reflections are then miscommunicating the tacit and often-oblique language of experiences in dancing: they "de-scribe" or "sub-scribe" what is instantaneous and spontaneous. Through dancing as research, we wish to expand and speed-up our awareness to grasp the moment of recognition, to grasp beauty in dance and choreography.

I believe that human nervous systems are neither fast nor direct enough to consciously grasp, contain, or direct improvised dancing in its high-speed transformations. These observations confirmed my interest in experimenting through *Nervous Systems* with alternative feedback models that do not alter the medium and follow the principles and rhythm of improvised dance. Accordingly, it is my aim to further research *Nervous Systems* and explore how human physiology can be extended in order not to pose a limit for this dance research practice. My next step in the research is to experiment with extending the nervous systems of the participants in order to come closer to an instantaneous grasp of the dance and choreographic materials. Through integrating artificial intelligence, as implemented in the field of algorithmic choreography, *Nervous Systems* extends the cognition of the dancing body and generates a feedback system that runs simultaneously with the improvisation. This experimental method, which I named *Somatic R.E.A.Ch. (research in electronic and algorithmic choreography)*, detects and processes the movement and speech of the dancer digitally during his/her/their improvisation, in order to send it immediately back to the experimentation with movement through audio or visual devices.[4]

Nevertheless, this next phase in my research does not exclude the reporting activity of *Nervous Systems*. I consider storytelling and the recollecting of experience good ways of supporting and motivating us to further explore and reflect on what escapes our attention in dancing as a professional performer in Western theatre dance and dance improvisation culture.

---

4. "Thinking Bodies in Dance. A somatic R.E.A.Ch." is the title of my practice based PhD in the arts that I started in September 2020 at the Royal Conservatoire and the University of Antwerp. The goal of this research is to investigate how somatic practices *(Nervous Systems* in particular) and technology can mutually enhance each other in order to develop techniques for dance improvisation as research.

THE WAVE

A poetic documentation practice that consists of
collecting, arranging and removing stones in space.
An opportunity to consider a document as the process
of tasting the life span—emergence, persistence and
dissolution—of a collective event. A contemplative
experience based on paying attention to the spaces
in between perceptions, actions, objects and people.

Short description of Anouk Llaurens' practice as it appeared in the
...*Through Practices* program.

THE WAVE

Anouk Llaurens

This book chapter aims at sharing the practice of *THE WAVE* through two kinds of texts: an overview that the participants received before entering the practice and a reconstruction of the verbal guidance that was given while going through its protocol.

OVERVIEW

The practice unfolds in three two-hour phases—*the gathering, the forming,* and *the dissolution*—one for each day of the symposium. During each phase, participants perform the actions without talking. Communication happens through listening to presence and action in time/space.

Each day starts with the same guided preparation provided in order to open participants to a tactile and receptive experience of their surroundings. This introductory phase offers a perspective for understanding all senses—touch, hearing, smell, taste, and vision—as ultimately tactile.

These phases could be shortly described as follows:

The gathering: The group leaves the building in order to collect stones on the campus. Back in the space where the practice started, participants revisit their outdoor experience with their eyes closed. Then, they visualise throwing the collected stones onto an imaginary floor and look for words formed by the resulting constellation.

The forming: Participants write one of the words that appeared in the visualisation by laying out the collected stones on the concrete floor. Doing so, they pay attention to the global situation and to how they are writing their word in relation to the other people in the group. All words are organized around a cluster of seven flowerpots that will be used in a later phase as containers.

The dissolution: Participants undo the constellation of words by throwing each stone, aiming at the flowerpots. Words written with stones dissolve into their sound, as stones hit containers.

RECONSTRUCTION OF THE VERBAL GUIDANCE

(guided preparation)

Take two blankets, to lay on the floor. Pay attention to where you are placing yourself in relation to other people in the group. Focus your attention on your sensations. What emerges now as experience? What is present as body? What is present as environment?

…bring your attention to your breath. Where do you perceive its movement? The body is expanding, lightening up when you inhale; it meets the ground more intimately when you exhale. Pay attention to the space between inhalation and exhalation, and again between exhalation and inhalation…

…pay attention to your relation to the ground as you are breathing. How is the floor touching you? Touch is the mother of all senses. Smell, taste, hearing, and vision are tactile. The environment is touching you from all directions…

…let your breath open the pores of your skin. Sounds are touching you as well—sounds of the room, of other people, other practices, sounds of space inside and outside. Breathing. Sharing oxygen. Tasting the touch of light through the eyelids. Tasting space in between, in between sounds, smells, sensations, details.

The gathering

Take a paper bag, put your coat and shoes on, and follow me outside the building. We are going to flock in silence towards the grass, picking up stones and small objects on our path. The group can condense and expand in space...

...welcome the touch of present conditions. Your sensations are your guide. Let the warmth of the sun touch the skin of your face. Images are touching your retina. What do you see? What is calling you?

Pay attention to the sensation of the stone in your hand, its weight, its temperature. Is it smooth? Is it angular? How is your hand moulding around it? How is your whole body organized when you put it in your bag?

Remember the group. Where are the others? Zooming out now, tasting the space in between people, sensation of air, sounds. Breathing. Pay attention to the sensation of your shoulder appearing in response to the weight of your bag. There is endless time. We have a goal and we are focusing on the path...

...let your plan and action be redirected by present sensations. Breathing. Listen to the resonance of your actions. How are they affecting you and the global situation? Now the ringing bell informs you that it is the moment to return to the space. You have endless time. There is no time...

...we are back to the space. Put your bag next to the window and take a blanket to sit on. We can all sit in a circle. Your spine is upright now. Close your eyes and pay attention to your sensations. What is emerging as body and as environment? Pay attention to the movement of your breath. How is the floor, the room touching you now?

Take a moment to revisit your experience of gathering of stones and objects outside...

...what is still present from the previous experience? Do you see images? Is it kinaesthetic? Do you remember sound? Do you feel emotions? What do you think about? Do sensations manifest in a linear way, more fragmented, in disorder? Just take note without judging...

...imagine that you are throwing the collected stones on the floor, as if you would throw shells to read an oracle. What is the word formed by the constellation of stones? Take your time to let it emerge. Remember breathing, tasting your sensations. If there are several words appearing, choose one...

...take a marker and write the word on the window. Where do you want to write in relation to the global space and to the other words that are already written? Where you want to write it in relation to the global space and to the other words that are already written. What is the constellation of words emerging from the collective practice?

The forming

The clay pots mark the centre of a circular space. Take a bag and look at that space. There is endless time, there is no time...

...go to the area that is calling you. Let what you see, hear, and feel guide and redirect your steps. When you have found a place, start writing your word with the collected stones. As the space devoted to the practice is circular, there is no top or bottom; you can write the word in any direction, even change direction on the way...

...how far from the clay pots are you starting? Do you have a strategy in mind? How big do you imagine your word to be in relation to the whole constellation? Can you taste the presence of other people writing and the presence of words in progress? Pay attention to the collective choreography...

...take the time to experience the space in between stones, objects, and people. If you zoom in, you might taste the details of improbable assemblage. You can share your treasures and steal some from others. Everything is yours and nothing is yours...

...remember zooming out, expanding your awareness. Use the breath to open yourself to be lost, not knowing, not recognizing. Can you let go of your plan? Is it more appropriate to stick to it?

Are you rushing the process because you want to reach your goal? There is nowhere to go. Remember to breathe. Your sensations are your guide. When you are done, take the time to contemplate the collective constellation.

The dissolution

Today is the last day. We are undoing the constellation of words by throwing stones and objects into the clay pots that are at the centre. Take the time to contemplate what was constructed yesterday before we start undoing it. Let your curiosity and your sensations guide your steps...

...I invite you to pay special attention to the sound of the space and the sound of your actions today. We are undoing the constellation to create a soundscape together. Tasting the resonance of the different kinds

of stones and objects hitting the pots, the floor, the wall.
For how long do they resonate? Pay attention to the space
in between sounds. Remember silence…

…notice if you are becoming obsessed with being successful at aiming and forget about listening to the sounds.
What happens in the body when the stone misses its target?
Taste the sensation of your face, your jaw. Come back to
the collective soundscape. Take the time to zoom out and
appreciate the global situation. You don't have to be doing
all the time. What about being?

Pay attention to the duration of silence and sounds. What
is the sound of heaviness? What is the sound of lightness?
When a stone breaks a pot, how does this affect you? Where
does it resonate? What kind of emotion arises? Anger, sadness, joy? Pieces of broken pots and stones are now part of
the same crowd. Container and content are merging…

…keep listening to the soundscape. What if we are making
sound to reveal silence? Take the time to taste the quality
of silence. Pay attention to the lifespan of the collective
practice. Do you notice that the rhythm is regular now? Is
it a collective choice? Are you on automatic pilot? Let your
habits be disturbed by the present conditions. It is not about
knowing, but about learning. When you feel it is the end,
you can call "End!"…

    …remember silence.

FROM WHERE WE ARE

From Where We Are is a guided encounter with space. Based on a written protocol that is followed step by step, we construct and expose our invisible, intangible and subjective relations with the spatial environment, where the exercise takes place. Throughout the practice we build awareness and sensitivity for the concrete impact these relations can have on ourselves and also on the space that we are part of.

Short description of Miriam Rohde's & Laetitia Gendre's practice as it appeared in the ... *Through Practices* program.

An Exercise in Attachment

Laetitia Gendre
Miriam Rohde

"At least two entities have to arrive to create an encounter, a 'bringing forth' in the sense of an occupation. (…) The dash in 'co-incide', must be highlighted here to avoid turning the shared arrival into a matter of chance. To 'co-incide' suggests how different things happen at the same moment, a happening that brings things near to other things, whereby the nearness shapes the shape of each thing."

Sara Ahmed, Queer Phenomenology, 39

THE PHYSICAL THRESHOLD AT THE INVISIBLE DOOR

Back in October 2019, we walked through a wooden double-winged door into the multifunctional space of an art school: ground level, dark concrete flooring, windows all around except for one wood-paneled wall, metal gridded window shades, black, probably sound absorbing ceiling, six white mobile elements to be used as room dividers… a nondescript, somewhat generic surrounding. We had been invited to take part in the symposium … *Through Practices* and, together with the other invitees, we were now going to discover how to use, share, and appropriate this space, how to accommodate ourselves in it, become acquainted with its details, and get to know each other… before leaving it again in three days.

Writing this text, we enter the same space again, and you, in reading it, are about to join us. Together, we will encounter people and situations we remember. Just as one would rely on the details one recalls when visiting a place for a second time, we will assemble this text from the scattered material we have gathered during the symposium: our own fragmented memories and all the bits and pieces that have been brought in from other people; stories we have been told; comments we have received; conversations we have overheard; situations we have witnessed; statements that have been made; opinions that have been expressed; questions that have been asked... And while the text will take shape, the trail of our material's origins will get more and more lost and the identities of the author (or authors), the narrator (or narrators) and all protagonists will get ever more jumbled.

At first, you might be disoriented and only see some unconnected outlines, hardly visible contours, and fragments of information that do not make much sense at all. But little by little, as the paragraphs accumulate into a text, the space and a part of what has been taking place in it will appear in front of your eyes—just as the exercise only takes shape while doing it and is shaped by those who are doing it. Writing this text is like constructing an entrance. The text is the physical threshold of an invisible door, through which we can access and (re)encounter a space and time located in the past.

THE SPACE IN-BETWEEN THE HANDLE OF THE FIRE EXTINGUISHER

There are only two aspects of our exercise that have remained unchanged since we started working with it in 2016. The first one is the title *From where we are*. The second one is the fact that the entire four hours of one session are determined by a written protocol that the exercise meticulously follows. Before a session starts, a copy of this protocol is handed to all participants. They take turns reading it out loud and then follow each step. Right at the beginning, a crucial point of the protocol is explained: when you are asked to choose 'something' that is present in the space (i.e. visible, touchable, audible, or even imaginable from where you are sitting or standing), you should refer to this 'something' as an 'element.'

In the first of the three sessions that are scheduled for the symposium, someone presents a fire extinguisher as one of the five elements each participant has to choose. We pause and start to inquire: what do you mean exactly? Do you want to select the whole fire extinguisher? Or do you only mean its metal parts? Or the details made of plastic? Or rather its content (which of course we cannot see but we know must be inside the metal casing)? Or its colour? Or only its shiny powder coating (without any colour whatsoever)? In the end, the participant revised his decision and selected the space in between the handle of the fire extinguisher.

To make such a choice would probably not have been possible without giving the fire extinguisher a break from being a 'fire extinguisher' and instead starting to disassemble the object into its various components. To 'take something apart' relates to the etymological meaning of the word "analysis," which is made up from *ana* "up, back, throughout" and *lyein* "to unfasten, loosen, divide, release." The analysis of an object opens up a realm of material and immaterial information. Textures, colours, light and shadow, movements, and sound can all become elements. The moment when the participants realize the immensity of possible choices while disassembling the objects around them is frequently met with excitement. Witnessing the disintegration (if only imagined) of a seemingly stable environment might satisfy our playful instincts, as well as a certain destructive impulse. It is as if a sort of tension was released, triggered by the sudden short-cutting of the obligation to make sense, to conform to the countless tacitly shared agreements and definitions our environment is held together by—what things are, what they are for, how they are embedded in their respective contexts, and what they mean to us.

THE CAMEMBERT OF LIGHT

The third and last session has started at 9am. We have already gone through the introduction of the protocol and are now at the point where the participants scan the room once again to select five elements that they want to work with over the next four hours. The group is small, which should accelerate the whole process but, instead, everyone seems eager to dig deeper into each task, pondering their words and decisions, asking questions, taking time to briefly discuss them. We usually try to avoid diverting from the protocol in order not to break the flow and the concentration, pointing out to the participants that at the very end of the exercise there will be a moment for common reflection. But this time, breaking the rules seems appropriate, as it plays into the intimate and relaxed atmosphere of the moment. The low morning sun is sifting through the grid of the metal window shades into the room, streaking across the concrete floor. By the surrounding buildings, the light is partially cut out, which in some places creates an effect of immaterial floaty three-dimensional shapes that fill the space. One participant selects such a slice of sunlight as one of her elements. While she tries to find the right words to share her choice with the group, it once again becomes clear how difficult it can be to achieve a degree of precision needed to make a selected element accessible to others. Different elements—material-immaterial, big-small, ephemeral or not, and so forth—ask for different approaches to precision... When the woman guides the group to carefully approach the chosen shape of light for closer inspection, she suddenly blurts out, "why, don't you get it, I mean this slice of light that looks like a piece of a camembert!" And immediately everyone else can see it, too. The transition from many descriptive words to one well-chosen nickname can help to generate an image that unlocks a common visual library in which we seem to move more quickly and smoothly than in a realm of letters and words.

I remember how the 'camembert of light,' the position of which depended on the fluctuating and slowly disappearing sunlight, was moving at a very low speed through the space, but somehow kept its trademark form for a long time. I also remember the pleasure of walking through it, sitting and standing in it, stepping into and out of it. How funny, strange, and beautiful to picture it at this very moment in the late morning, on its daily trajectory through the part of the space in which we then worked, being ephemeral and stable at the same time.

J'S HAIR, A'S HAND...
ALL THAT IS YELLOW

At one point in the protocol, the participants are handed a stack of cards with tasks that they have to commonly follow. At the beginning, the questions seem simplistic and absurd to many. But soon people find themselves immersed in heated discussions or silent and concentrated contemplation. "Arrange your drawings according to the size of your chosen elements." "Arrange your drawings according to the weight of your elements." "Try out a sound for each element you have chosen." "Arrange your drawings to the degree of mobility of your elements."

What sounds easy in the beginning gradually confronts us with the complexity of our choices. How stable is a patch of light that disappears each time that a cloud covers the sun but reappears everyday throughout the years when the sun is shining? How would you adapt your definition of weight with regard to an element such as the distance between two people? And what does a category such as 'everything that is yellow' do to your idea of size? In all these examples, the attention is not directed towards the elements themselves, but rather towards their incidental characteristics, among all of which 'time' is probably the most significant.

Once the temporal depth is added, space feels more like an assemblage of features: materials, movements, phenomena, relations, rhythms.

THE FEAR OF STANDING ON TOP OF THE LADDER

Throughout the exercise, the amount of information the participants work with is constantly growing, until the flux of impressions that has to be retraced, remembered, reflected, related, compared again and again can create an abysmal feeling of getting ever more lost—a sort of vertigo, as if one was about to disappear in the vortex of one's own perception.

This point of information overdose and crumbling concentration usually occurs after two hours into the exercise. It is a moment that makes me think of a classical situation: I very uncomfortably stand at the top of a ladder and I really want to descend, but I am frozen in my position... The half-time break announced by the protocol is usually greeted with relief. To get everyone down from the top of this metaphorical ladder, and to relax the exhausted brains and bodies, we offer coffee, tea, nuts, and chocolate and we provide some background information about the exercise:

After one of our workshops, we recount, a participant sent us an essay by sociologist and philosopher Bruno Latour in which he develops some ideas that helped us to contextualize and fine-tune our proposition.[1] The essay opens with a comic strip of "Mafalda" who dryly suggests to her father, sitting relaxed in his recliner smoking a cigarette, that his cigarette is probably smoking him (and not vice versa).[2] Whereupon the father frantically destroys the remaining cigarettes in the package. Latour explicates:

---

1. Bruno Latour, "Factures / Fractures: from the concept of network to the concept of attachment," Anthropology and Aesthetics, no. 36 (Autumn, 1999). https://www.jstor.org/stable/i20167471. [Accessed April 18 2020]

> "From the active form (I smoke a cigarette) to the passive form (you are smoked by a cigarette) nothing has changed other than the apportionment of master and instrument: The father alternates too drastically from one opposition to another: too comfortable in the first images, too panicked in the last. What if the question rested instead on the absence of mastery, on the incapacity (either in the active or a passive way) to define our attachments? How can we speak with precision of what the Greek call 'the middle voice', the verb that is neither active nor passive?"

Instead of clinging to the paradigms of master-slave, active-passive, using-being used, controlling-being controlled, Latour introduces the term *"faire faire"* which means "to make one do" or "causing to be done." He suggests that "doing" (acting, creating etc.) cannot be thought of as a singular act, but is always linked to something that has been done before and that will enable something else to be done or happen afterwards. The question 'Who controls and who is controlled?' is replaced by the question 'What are we attached to?,' because, he argues, it is rather the fact that we are attached (or not) that makes us do things (or not). For Latour, attachment stems from "the formidable proliferation of objects, properties, beings, fears, techniques... that make us do things unto others." In our words, attachment is brought about by a complex, beautiful, surprising, uncontrollable entanglement of material and immaterial aspects through which action upon action unfolds.

2. "Mafalda" is a comic strip by Argentinian illustrator Quino that ran from 1964-1973.

THE FICTITIOUS IMAGE OF MYSELF ON TOP OF THE STAIRS

In reference to the above notion, the last step of the protocol is called "faire-faire." For this step, the protocol provides a time of 30 minutes, longer than for any other task. We point out that there is no obligation to act: "don't break your head over finding an idea or being original." So, people sit around, ponder their elements one last time, and wait. Now and then, a participant makes a move toward one of their elements and interacts with it in one way or the other.

During one of our sessions, a participant chooses as an element: 'the fictitious image of myself on top of the stairs.' Once stated, the element is collectively accepted as spatially present. But, its purely imaginary nature confronts us with difficulties when it comes to engaging with this last step... Examples of situations where fictional images, as one could say, 'make us do' things can easily be found: for instance, education or social mimicry foster processes of identification with invented characters or role models. In this case, these processes can be fueled by narratives, while 'the fictitious image of myself on top of the stairs' remains a 'flat' mental image, like a slide inserted into the space. This may be a cause for the elusiveness of the relation. Lending depth to the image could facilitate interaction: 'the fictitious image of myself on top of the stairs' could be me as a ghostly doppelganger, or the projection of my desire to be elsewhere...

At one point in the symposium, I also encountered these difficulties with reacting to a self-generated mental image. While participating in another practice, I am asked to imagine—eyes closed—throwing stones on the ground. Starting from this imaginary action, I am asked to let words emerge, and then write them with a marker pencil on a windowpane in order to use them for the next part of the exercise. I feel focused, ready to dedicate all my brain power to the task. But as my mind is trying hard to picture

the stones, shapes, colours, and textures are shifting
constantly without any possibility to choose a few
and stop the flow. It's also proving difficult to imagine
the act itself, the gesture, the sounds it makes. Things
remain weightless; flimsy images keep bouncing against
each other without any result... After a few minutes,
it is clear that no word is coming out. When someone
amongst us rushes through the space, grabs one of the
buckets full of stones and vigorously spills its content
on the floor, I feel instantly released, equally astonished
and amused. And I have a word.

THE TEXTURE OF MY OWN BLANKET

All the participants in the symposium gather twice a
day for morning and evening meetings on a beautiful
round carpet.[3] As soon as it is unrolled, the colourful
island floating on the plain concrete surface creates a
warm spot with an almost magnetic power of attraction.
The carpet evokes these cosmological representations
organized in concentric circles that refer to natural
elements: a marbled yellow and orange magma in the
middle, layers of brown earthy crust, a large azure circle
streaked by lightning which fuses from the last white
and fluffy circle. Most people take their shoes off and sit
or lie down, and it feels completely natural to take part
in the discussions while stretching one's legs or fiddling
with the wool. I am sitting cross-legged, sipping my
coffee, enjoying the pleasure of being, not only visually,
but also physically, immersed in this image, observing
this unusual combination of looking and moving.

The distinction between these two activities
('seeing' and 'doing') was also at the heart of the questions we asked ourselves when we started to develop

---

3. The carpet is part of an artistic research project by
Clémentine Vaultier, 2019.

the exercise. Our purpose was to broaden the ability to perceive and concretely react and yet, in the beginning, the practice was almost purely visual and cerebral: looking, choosing, discussing, writing—everything was done 'comfortably sitting' (as said in the protocol) from the position one had chosen in the space. It took us some time to find out how movement, body, and action could be integrated into the protocol. This got resolved when we started considering the act of looking as a practice in itself that fully engages our cognitive faculties and plays an effective role when it comes to taking action. The general mistrust of everything 'visual' (and its supposed tendency to keep us on the surface of things) is deeply rooted in the Platonic renunciation of all kinds of representations, whether pictorial or theatrical. "To be a spectator is to be separated from both the capacity to know and the power to act", writes Rancière. He continues his argumentation:

> "Emancipation begins when we challenge the opposition between viewing and acting; when we understand that the self-evident facts that structure the relations between saying, seeing and doing themselves belong to the structure of domination and subjection. It begins when we understand that viewing is also an action that confirms or transforms this distribution of positions. The spectator also acts, like the pupil or scholar. She observes, selects, compares, interprets. She links what she sees to a host of other things that she has seen on other stages, in other kinds of places."[4]

Even if our exercise does not reproduce the configuration of a theatrical device (we are neither 'spectators' nor 'actors' in this space, and it is not strictly speaking a 'performance'),

---

4. Jacques Rancière, The emancipated Spectator (London: Verso, 2011), 13.

From where we are is based on the same emancipatory aspiration to shift the thin dividing lines that organize our representations of what is present with and around us. Our exercise, in this sense, is located somewhere between structure and appearance, between tangible materiality and imagination.

THE EMERGENCY EXIT SIGN, BUT ONLY THE PARTS THAT ARE NOT COVERED WITH BLACK TAPE

This is maybe a good moment to pause, turn around, and gather again at the departure point from which we started writing and you started reading this text. We stand in front of the entrance to a space at another moment in time, an invisible door. But before we step over its physical threshold and leave the space we encountered behind, please bring your attention to a piece of paper over there, next to the doorframe. If you come closer, you can read the following words:

> "Simultaneous arrivals are not necessarily a matter of chance; arrivals are determined, at least in a certain way, as a determination that might determine what gets near, even if it does not decide what happens **once we are near.** If being near to this or that object is not a matter of chance, what happens in the "now" of this nearness remains open, in the sense that we don't always know how things affect each other, or how we will be affected by things."[5]

What's that look on your faces? Are you asking where we actually are? Do you want to know who this group of people is and why you are here? Is this a game

---

5. Sara Ahmed, Queer Phenomenology: Orientations, Objects, Others, (Durham NC: Duke University Press, 2006), 39.

of manipulation? Would you like to know how to get out of here? I see someone turning her head. She points to an emergency exit sign above another door and determinately walks towards it. She climbs on two stacked beer crates in order to inspect and touch the sign, tilts her head, and seems to contemplate the sign for a moment. Then she swiftly turns around and shouts in our direction: "I take the emergency exit sign, but only the parts that are not covered with black tape."

GROUP SERVICE

We are always already taking decisions when feeding ourselves. *Group Service* will be based on the decisions taken in the early morning at the food-bank. It is the practice that will feed guides, hosts and those who join and is dependant on the time that can go into food production. You are invited to join both the decision-making and the cooking process in the early morning and throughout the day.

Short description of Bilal Kamilla Arnout's practice as it appeared in the ... *Through Practices* program.

(No) Vision on Eating and Drinking

Bilal Kamilla Arnout

Ben een deel van het probleem,
eet vaak vis en te veel vlees /
Vlieg over heel de wereld alsof dat het mij niks scheelt /
M'n wagen is verkocht maar
zit nog veel te vaak in Ubers /
Nog altijd niets gekocht en ik maak deel uit
van de huurders.[1]

---

1. Zwangere Guy, Grijze Zone #1 on Brutaal, Topnotch – 083.647-1, CD (2019). Freely translation by myself: *Am part of da problem, often eat fish and too much meat / Fly over the globe as if I don't give a damm / My car is sold but hang in Ubers too often still / Still no house bought and just one of those renting.*

From: heike_langsdorf <heike.langsdorf@me.com>
Date: Friday, 3 April 2020 at 14:13
To: "bilal.alnouri@gmail.com" <bilal.alnouri@gmail.com>

Dear Bilal,

Chatting and listening to you via Facebook messenger,
I have the feeling that you are not doing so well.
    The last deadline for contributing to the fifth book
of the series *Choreography as Conditioning* has passed.
    Still, we want to see how your 'vision' can become
part of our bundle of texts.
    I will attach what you told me and sent me thus far.
And maybe you will just reply once and that's it.

This 'poor correspondence' might just show that
feeling well and being productive are not always given.
Nevertheless, there are some precious thoughts to be
maintained, sustained, or suspended.

You sent me this fragment a long time ago:

> *On Eating and Drinking*
>
> *Then an old man, a keeper of an inn, said,*
> *Speak to us of Eating and Drinking.*
>
> *And he said:*
>
> *Would that you could live on the fragrance of the*
> *earth, and like an air plant be sustained by the light.*
>
> *But since you must kill to eat, and rob the newborn*
> *of its mother's milk to quench your thirst, let it then*
> *be an act of worship.*

> *And let your board stand an altar on which the pure and the innocent of forest and plain are sacrificed for that which is purer and still more innocent in man.*[2]

… and you told me how difficult it was to find a way of proceeding within the context of my invitation. Engaging in our breakfast group conversation on the round carpet, this question had become pertinent:[3] whether or not to kill and eat the rooster, living on the campus? During the second day of … *Through Practices,* you continued speculating on how we, as a group, would handle the issue that filled our mornings:

At that moment, the animal had become a threat to all other chickens and roosters due to its increasing aggression.

You predicted, when we were talking casually (off the carpet) that we would not eat the rooster. As a group we would not be ready to decide for or against the killing. One thing the group had agreed on though was this: if we would eat him, we would need to kill him ourselves.

You assumed that this 'killing' would follow those who were interested beyond … *Through Practices*. But if we would eat the rooster before the fifth book would be launched, you would propose to add one feather to each to the 500 copies. We looked at each other and wondered how many feathers a rooster might have. And we remembered that someone told us that the most awkward part of killing and preparing a chicken for consumption is the ripping off of the feathers. Ouch!

I send you here the little correspondence we had with the dean of the school. What if you read it and offered an end?

2. Kahlil Gibran, The Prophet and Other Tales (San Diego: Canterbury Classics, 2019), 125.
3. This carpet is is a work by Clementine Vauldetier (2019) and considered by her a mobile gathering space.

From: heike_langsdorf <heike.langsdorf@me.com>
Date: Monday, 28 October 2019 at 17:18
To: Lars Kwakkenbos <lars.kwakkenbos@hogent.be>, "bilal.alnouri@gmail.com"
<bilal.alnouri@gmail.com>, "elowise@radical-hope.be"
<elowise@radical-hope.be>
Subject: Eating the Rooster?

Dear Lars,

What I could find out is that if the rooster belongs to someone, that person can give permission to kill the animal (or kill it themself).
    Secondly, one needs to make sure that nobody is surprised or shocked because they were not informed about the 'slaughtering situation' going on.

The second issue we can take care of.
    As for making sure that the rooster belongs to someone, how could we arrange this?

Could you, Lars, become the owner?
Could the rooster be 'donated' to Bilal personally?

It is not yet sure whether the rooster will actually get killed.

I just want to make sure that if we would collectively decide to eat him, the situation is clarified in advance.

Thank you!

    Heike

From: Lars Kwakkenbos <lars.kwakkenbos@hogent.be>
Date: 28 October 2019 at 21:20:19 GMT+1
To: heike_langsdorf <heike.langsdorf@me.com>, "bilal.alnouri@gmail.com" <bilal.alnouri@gmail.com>, "elowise@radical-hope.be" <elowise@radical-hope.be>
Cc: Ilse Den Hond <ilse.denhond@hogent.be>
Subject: Re: Eating the Rooster?

Dear Heike, Bilal and Elowise,

I would like to present the case to someone who knows the law in detail. Frederik Swennen of the Universiteit Antwerpen does, I think. If you send me a detailed plan of what will happen, I am willing to contact him. Up until now, I see four questions that need to be answered by him:

> First question: who does a rooster living in the school belong to?
>
> Second: can someone find the rooster and claim it as a property?
>
> Third: can you kill the rooster within the context of an artistic project, even if you decide this collectively (who is the collective?) and eat it?
>
> Fourth: if so, how should you kill it?

I also put Ilse Den Hond, our communications manager, in cc, because we have needed specific communication strategies for similar issues in the past, so I'd prefer to keep her updated as well.

> All best Lars

From: Heike Langsdorf <heike.langsdorf@me.com>
Date: 29 October 2019 at 06:27:38 GMT+1
To: Lars Kwakkenbos <lars.kwakkenbos@hogent.be>
Cc: "bilal.alnouri@gmail.com" <bilal.alnouri@gmail.com>,
"elowise@radical-hope.be" <elowise@radical-hope.be>,
Ilse Den Hond <ilse.denhond@hogent.be>
Subject: Re: Eating the Rooster?

Good Morning,

We will look at your questions during our 'Decisions at the Food Bank' session (8u – 9u) at Zwarte Zaal.

Feel warmly invited to join!

A little breakfast will be served there…

    Heike, Bilal, Elowise

From: bilal.alnouri@gmail.com <bilal.alnouri@gmail.com>
Date: Saturday, 13 June 2020 at 16:00
To: heike_langsdorf <heike.langsdorf@me.com>
Subject: Text

Hey Heike,

Yes, I want to bring this thread of thoughts, this text, to an end! I visited you on Friday. We were sitting on your terrace in Brussels. We talked about what to add to the existing two elements of my contribution.

There is the email correspondence between us and the institution dating from October 2019, and a prayer I wrote recently.

I now add what I think needs to be added in order to have a comprehensive read…

Working with Barbara Raes and you two years ago in the context of Open End,[4] while I was living at KASK with a little newborn lamb, I started to let myself be guided by a question: what could living with an animal make us witness and learn about ourselves? What can we learn about how we get the food we need and about how life needs to be nourished by life?

What I haven't yet figured out is how to proceed in order to incorporate these questions into my work as an artist. When you asked me to take part in …*Through Practices,* I first panicked. What is my practice for God's sake? Eventually, I came to think about my practice as a cook. But, what sort of cook had I been until then? So far, I just arranged ingredients in such a way that people found the results tasty.

---

4. *Open End,* (23 October - 17 November 2017), a workshop by Barbara Raes (in the context of her project *Beyond the Spoken—workplace for unacknowledged loss),* proposed to and run by Autonomous Design at KASK School of Arts Hogent.

So, I decided to invite someone who I would call
a real cook. His work starts before something is declared as
an ingredient. In this sense, facing the production of meat
he always says: "There are in general—and unfortunately—
two extreme types: those who farm and 'produce animals'
but cannot even think about seeing them slaughtered, and
others that kill numbly." How can we deal with this unquestioned disconnection between the 'production of life'
and the act of killing?

For ... *Through Practices,* I proposed more or less this:
a number of edible things and us, a group of people that
needs to eat and therefore has to decide what is edible and
what and how to eat. Starting with wood and fire in the
garden, the idea was that we have to manage together how
to eat. If food would not be enough or too burnt, we could
just grab something on our own costs in the Cafeteria of
KASK. But after this experience, what still concerns me are
the unresolved questions we discussed: why and how to kill
the rooster?

Since I haven't found an answer to this question,
I would like to contribute to this book by formulating an
intention and a prayer. The intention is to kill and eat the
rooster with a group of people who want to go through this
process with me before this book is launched. If we manage
to do it, we will pluck the rooster and stick one feather in
each of the 500 copies; if not, we will collect the feathers
which chicks naturally lose, and add one to each book.

I will email you the reworked prayer!

      Bilal

From: Bilal Alnouri <bilal.alnouri@gmail.com>
Date: Tuesday, 16 June 2020 at 22:28:51 GMT+1
To: Heike Langsdorf <heike.langsdorf@me.com>
Subject: new poem

Hey Heike,

I tried to make it clearer. It is simple and became a mix between the two prayers I had in mind previously.

Gooooood Night!

In the land of me
I walk so free
under my feet grass green
around me trees stand still
vegetable and fruit spread ready to pick.

> *In the land of me*
> *chickens are running free*
> *between two roosters fighting for the lead*
> *certainly one must go out of the field.*

In the land of me
there is not only me
other people gather with a hope for good meal
stick stones and fire started warm
the question has been asked
should we put the roster on?

In the land of me
company stores are not far a walk
too much meat standing on the shelves
waiting for us to pick free from guilt,
free from touch
in plastic bags and with a valid day,
everything is so clean.

In the land of me
I am not any more so free
to take out feathers and bones on my own
is it a question of not killing more
or all the worshiping today most have a code.

In the land of me
maybe there is another way of doing
doing it together
put our thoughts on the table
maybe put them in the fire or even on an altar
there is no alternative
there is no vision
stop questioning offices and ownership
just be conscious
improve each other's death
and accept each other's lives.

P.S.
"It is often nature itself that inspires me to make a new work. As in 2008: during a skirmish in our yard, a spur breaks off of one of the cocks, a Malinois owl beard. He is therefore no longer taken seriously, he lost status, he is expelled. The rooster has lost its pride and becomes lonely. I set him aside: it got too sad to look at."[5]

In the end of (No) Vision, there is No (Vision) and there is (No) dead chicken. However, adding feathers to our book will bear new life and value.

Although I am not a religious man, I believe in the power of rituals. Inshallah.

---

5. Koen Vanmechelen and Geerdt Magiels. *This is not a Chicken*, (Leuven: LannooCampus, 2020), 97. Freely translated by myself.

ROOM OF CONSTELLATIONS

Linger on. Leave a note. Associate.
What can we find out about the relationship between spatial conditions, thinking and writing? This room is a spatial-temporal figure, a punctuation in space and time, it can be at once a contemplative space and a gathering practice. A 'temporal bracket' to where to withdraw and from where to restart your involvement in the present practices. How do they look and sound from a distance? How is this different to indulging in them?

Short description of Irene Lehmann's practice as it appeared in the
...*Through Practices* program.

Space between actions: Reflections on *room of constellations*, a research environment

Irene Lehmann

ACCUMULATIONS

On the afternoon of the second day of ... *Through Practices* I considered tearing down the walls of *room of constellations* in order to open it spatially to the other ongoing practices.[1]

However, before following through with this idea, I noticed someone sleeping in the room, and since this was not the first time this had happened, I hesitated. When some participants of the event later told me that they experienced a strong feeling of comfort from the room's presence, regardless of whether or not they entered it, I started to suspect a 'somatic necessity' of the room. The sleeping and the verbal reactions revealed an unexpected comforting air that made me reconsider tearing down the walls.

Instead, on the third day, a different possibility of connecting emerged through a participant jotting down notes and drawings from a discussion that was part of the *dance of the day* practice.[2] Through making use of the set-up of the *eyes can touch* practice, her notes became visible while writing.[3] This spontaneous recording of the transitory moments in which action, interaction, and reflection take place reverberated with my initial idea of creating the *room of constellations*. In addition to the spontaneous transformation of kinetic actions and perceptions into words, I created this room as a space set apart from the other practices,

[1]. *Room of constellations* was basically a defined space, set spatially apart from other ongoing practices. This text tries to unfold its different aspects, meanings, and relations within the framework of the ... *Through Practices* Symposium and to previous research environments.
[2]. *Dance of the day*, by Heike Langsdorf.
[3]. *Eyes can touch*, installation by Miriam Rohde and Laetitia Grande. This practice made a camera and a beamer film hands drawing on papers on a table and simultaneously projecting them to a wall facing the person on the table.

simultaneously investigating the movement of withdrawing as a counterpart to immersion which is related to my usual research practice as a researcher in the humanities.[4] Furthermore, *room of constellations* was a space in which to bring 'home' notes, fragments, and findings from any field research and to arrange them in a way that both enables their meanings to emerge and goes beyond typical scientific procedures. The space is defined by detecting concealed connections and patterns formed by the fragments. An underlying assumption in *room of constellation's* conception was that research is partly an unpredictable process and sometimes lucky moments occur when answers emerge despite the fact that one was not actively looking for them.

With *room of constellations,* I started to investigate an academic research practice, which I encountered first in my own procedures. Later, it turned out that its variations are widespread, but seldomly discussed. My practice is based on a critical hermeneutic tradition that originated during the Late German Enlightenment and continues in Walter Benjamin's writings.[5] The practice consists of two main elements: the circular movement between immersion and withdrawal, and practices of collecting fragments of thoughts.[6] Since both elements are modes of spatial thinking, I started to ponder other such physical spaces of research, such as study centers, libraries, and archives. Dance philosopher Susan Leigh Foster reveals how theory as thought-movement is related to physical movement, as well as to conversations with other theorists/researchers.[7]

---

4. My main occupation as a theatre scholar turns the performative space often into a space where my field research takes place.
5. Thomas Regehly, "'Kannitverstan' – Benjamin, Hebel und die Hermeneutik," in Was nie geschrieben wurde, lesen. Frankfurter Benjamin-Vorträge, eds. Lorenz Jäger and Thomas Regehly (Bielefeld: Aisthesis, 1992), 59-95.
6. I refer here to the hermeneutic circle: a thought movement between different elements and layers that add and change meaning with each 'circle'.

While possibilities for the fragile practices of thinking together as a part of theorizing are diminishing in a fragmented academic system that puts competition above cooperation,[8] although the wish to bridge communicational gaps with non-academics and those specializing in other topics is often articulated. At a certain point of understanding what constitutes the dynamics and quality of each research process, discussing thought and knowledge organization with others has opened up as a possibility for me. It then turned out that sharing the fascination of auratic archive objects and undecipherable manuscripts, and of meeting reluctant librarians was an essential part of *doing* research. I noticed that since this practical, orally transmitted knowledge rarely becomes part of any academic essay, it creates a sort of complementary, or shadow knowledge, or a counter-figure, to put it in aesthetic terms. *Room of constellation* was set up to investigate some of the many shadows that are created during multifaceted research processes.

SUSPENDED SYNTHESIS

Room of constellations offered a space for participants to *leave notes,* to *associate,* or to just *linger* and let impressions sink in.[9] I deliberately tried to avoid a score that would produce the fetishized appearance of linear, subsequent actions and causal/logical results.[10]

7. Susan Leigh Foster, "Dancing and Theorizing and Theorizing Dancing," in Dance [and] Theory, eds. Gabriele Brandstetter and Gabriele Klein (Bielefeld: transcript, 2013), 19-32, here 19. Foster traces theory's meaning in ancient Greece: travelling, attending a theatre or sport spectacle, returning and exchanging with other 'theorists', establishing meaning through that interlocution (ibid.).
8. See: Nussbaum, Martha, Not for Profit. Why Democracy needs the Humanities. (Princeton NJ: Princeton University Press, 2010).
9. The three terms were the only instructions for using the *room of constellations*.

In addition to the possibility of fixing notes and drawings to the walls, an empty notebook offered an even more secluded space for contributing shorter records of situations of spatial thinking.[11] Both possibilities led to astonishing disclosures: stories about thoughts being caught or lost in different places like the liminal space between train stations or in one of the participant's bodies; drawings about overcoming the fear of making mistakes, or about the beauty of experiencing light each day. Additionally, words and phrases that came up during the days of *through practices* were taped to the walls. In this way, participants combined their thought fragments with those of others. Through the bodily and spatial practice of fixing scraps to the walls, visual patterns emerged: a sign of collective associating and thinking.

Critical hermeneutics entertains the notion that the human mind is not able to grasp the 'whole' of any given object: its cognizance can only occur through approximation, which leads to a constant changing of perspective in order to gain pieces that finally lead to a construction of the object. This process thus unfolds as a phenomenon of interference between the thinking person and their ability to perceive traces of meaning captivated in the fragments. The idea of approximation can not only be found in the concept of constellation as laid out by Walter Benjamin, but also offers a way to navigate the event of … *Through practices*. There, participants experienced a research framework together and individual—a framework made of practices that exist on their own and in dynamic relations with each other that created experiences and reflections, as well as insights and feelings.

10. Linearity is often linked to causality, but this doesn't imply that any score with subsequent actions follows that kind of logic.
11. *Stories of spatial thinking* was the title of the notebook laid out in the room. I wrote down some of the stories I was told by fellow researchers on different occasions. Participants wrote down their individual stories, thereby exploring what spatial thinking might mean to them.

NEGATIVE SPACES

From one of the discussions during the *dance of the day* practice the following phrase arose: "in the space between actions... we start sense making." While, in this context, 'actions' were mostly spontaneously created movements, I found a clue to the meaning of the constellational aspect in my own practice. In relation to movement, a 'space between actions' allows for a moment of suspension; in music it can be experienced during moments of silence. This interruptions, suspensions might be loaded with tensions that can either resolve with the resuming of the music's flow, or can be loaded with sheer unbearable doubts about whether the musical coherence is forever faded and torn apart.[12] Moments of simultaneity, interlacing, and polyphony[13] appeared not only in the *room of constellations* but also between the different practices of ... *Through practices*. *Room of constellations* was set apart visually from the other practices, yet it remained permeable to listening, as one person expressed on a pinned note: "Nobody sees me listening to the different sound spheres happening simultaneously. Practicing listening simultaneously." Listening simultaneously points to polyphonic listening and to a further layer of the 'space between...' phenomenon that occurred through the presence of different languages being spoken in the space. They created interfering layers of phonemes that could belong to multiple languages, thus allowing for

---

12. Regine Elzenheimer, Pause, Schweigen, Stille. Dramaturgien der Abwesenheit im postdramatischen Musik – Theater (Würzburg: Königshausen&Neumann, 2008).
13. The term polyphony is defined through compositional practices in 20th century music as the simultaneity of different and autonomous 'voices.' Literature theory scholar Michail Bachtin developed a similar concept of 'polyphony' in literary texts; see Michail M. Bachtin, Chronotopos (Frankfurt/Main: Suhrkamp, 2008).

multidirectional associations, detours, and new expressions in the participant's generally not native English.

A very interesting dynamic arose on the third day of the symposium that created a kind of density, in which meaning was overwritten and effaced. At this point, I'd like to return for a moment to the sleeping person I encountered in the *room of constellations*. From a distance, she appears to me as a figure of expression, an allegory for the essential shadow moments in the research process in and beyond ... *Through practices*. By sleeping, she defended the need for calm and empty spaces, for breathing and reproduction as integral to any production.[14] In academia and the arts, the spaces between actions are ever more reduced: too much is written, too many pieces are staged, while the needed space to rest, to experiment, and to associate freely fades away.

With special thanks to Kristina Odenweller, Britta Günther and all ... *through practitioners*.

---

14. See Karl Marx on the political and structural separation of what is defined as production in negating or subordinating all activities defined as reproduction. Karl Marx, Das Kapital. Kritik der politischen Ökonomie. 3 vol., =MEW Bd. 23-25 (Berlin: Dietz, 1979). See for instance vol.1, 230f.

1. A praxis is an exercise driven by a reflection. I present my notes
   on ... *Through Practices* as a dedicated witness. I try
   to practice a way of cutting into a space of uncertainty,
   exploring what I can unfold/fold-out by playing with
   different ideas about the mi-lieu, the middle space,
   the space of 'uncertainty,' a tension/attention...

A Praxis.
Cut-in/Fold-out [1]

Anne Dekerk

> "Pedagogy, for Serres, is not about turning someone into a swimmer in order for someone to learn what is at the other shore. This, indeed, would be the learning imaginary of an analytical pedagogy that shapes and gives direction to the learner. Serres instead seeks to articulate what happens in the middle, the moment of exposure or the present moment—in the middle of the river—where all directions are possible. Exactly this mi-lieu, this middle or third place is the time and space where freedom is undefined ('no direction') but possible to be defined ('to find all directions')." [2]

My score: look for the 'mi-lieu' as a dedicated witness. I like the fact that 'milieu' means 'the middle' as well as 'environment'.

I enter the space of a round carpet. I love round spaces. But they are deceptive.

How to receive someone in this space? How to 'program' coincidence? How to create spheres that cause accidental encounters and provoke unexpected meaning? How to have encounters, where the unmeasurable and the not-knowing appear?

Through practicing, we take the risk of transforming our 'self.' It is an invitation, a public gesture. [3] Is it possible to cut into something with your attention and unfold what transformed because of this attention?

---

2. Maarten Simons and Jan Masschelein, School, pedagogy and Foucault's undefined work of freedom. PDF file. April 25, 2019. https://respaedagogica.be/pub/school-pedagogy-and-foucaults-undefined-work-freedom.
3. I like to refer to Foucault who described his books not as a way of passing on knowledge and putting the reader into a position of ignorance, but as invitations and public gestures around which people can share experiences.

EARLY MORNING: DECISIONS AT THE FOOD BANK.

"If you want to eat it, you have to kill it.
If you can't kill it, don't eat it."[4]

Where does the rooster living here come from?
    The rooster is a sacred animal in a lot of cultures and is deeply embedded within some religious belief systems.

"Spirituality is structure."[5]

A rooster: immediate senses, no representation. Administrative and juridical questions unfold around the possibilities of killing a rooster. How free are we? How free is the rooster? Are we allowed to kill it, and who is allowed to kill it? Is this a public space, a pedagogical space, an art space? How are the aspects of the space relevant to the killing of the rooster? The story of the rooster unfolds. The rooster as a witness…

"Humans are practicing beings."[6]

I exit the space. I look at the space from the outside.
A charged space. A space which is in *waiting,* containing the *not foreseen*. I presume that a lot of words relating to *visual* aspects of witnessing will be present, as there is a certain dominance of the visual and the analytical.
    I look for something to hold on to. I enter again with the flyer, which contains a plan and timetable.
This provides my 'structure.' I look at the space and see how different spheres move and change in it. It is a field of transference, a case of projecting our (un)conscious desires.

---

4. Somebody around the carpet is quoting Joseph Beuys saying this.
5. Tina Vervaeke during a family constellation practice session, 2020, Menas, Belgium.
6. Peter Sloterdijk, You must change your life, on antropotechnics (Cambridge: Polity Press, 2014).

Waiting until something invokes me. Realizing that what invokes you is always already within you. I want no distance. I try to localize myself in a space. Finding measurable distances, making movements between near and far. If there is a centre, I can always be at a measurable distance from it. But these spheres evolve, implode, explode, and shift into one another. There is no centre. It is not possible to measure.

> FROM WHERE WE ARE.

I choose a practice with a duration of four hours. I choose to engage myself in this space. We proceed following a protocol/structure. A four hour commitment to the space. Time and space become elastic. I immerse myself in the performance of the protocol and cut into layers of space. So many invisible layers, walls, corners belong to this space. *Invisibility.*

Sometimes we touch, sometimes there are overlaps in space and sound with other practices and witnesses. *Mixing,* the practice of Fransien van der Putt plays with these overlaps in sound whilst we are practicing in the space. Spheres sharing walls. I forget I am a witness. I find. I build. I rebuild the space. I am built.

The longer you investigate an element of the space, the longer you get attached to it. This form of attachment is tied to engagement. You get intertwined with subjective aspects of the space.

How deep does this space go?

We might cut further into the space and deepen it through repetition.

> FOOD AND FIRE OUTSIDE:
> THE PRACTICE OF DAILY LIFE.

The rooster must be somewhere. I try to localize it. Is it watching me?

> "The voyage of children, that is the naked meaning of the Greek word pedagogy. Learning launches wandering."[7]

Waiting. Wandering. Failing. Attention deficit. Waiting. Wondering. No production of thoughts or meaning. At this moment, I am not consuming practices. Useless time (in terms of economics). I think contemporary pedagogical practices need more space for waiting, wandering, and uselessness. We need spaces in which to exercise boredom. We need spaces that don't exist to maximize people's capacities. We need places that remind us of the unspeakable and of our own death.

> Lost in space.
>
> Would someone witness how lost I am?
>
> Am I being lost in a dedicated way?

How many gradations of witnessing are there? Would we be able to make a witness spectrum? An attention spectrum? But this indeed would be a sign of wanting to grasp and measure our attention.

I have read that our attention span is only eight seconds long, since the introduction of smartphones. This is one second less than the attention of a goldfish, which lasts for nine seconds. A goldfish. Now we have a goldfish and a rooster.

We suffer a collective attention deficit disorder. Should pedagogy focus on practicing attention?

---

[7]. Maarten Simons and Jan Masschelein, School, pedagogy and Foucault's undefined work of freedom. PDF file. April 25, 2019. http://www. materialifoucaultiani.org/images/06simonsmasschelein.pdf.

FRAGILE COMMUNITY S/CORE.

Distance and proximity: the play of attachment? I come closer and closer to the practice. A practice you cannot register for as an audience. I ask permission to sit close to the table around which the practice evolves, physically joining the group. I remain silent. I am there. Just being present. I am only ear. Silent witness. I am conscious of being a presence. Conscious of the fact that my intense way of being attentive and the absence of my words intervenes in the ongoing practice.

What happens in between the witness and what is witnessed?

How does the attention of the witness influence the attention of other cohabitors of the space?

Gazes exchange. Non-verbal exchange. No words. Who witnesses the witness? How does the witness change what is witnessed and therefore co-create by being present?

I see a trace of someone who has been in this space. A small piece of bread. Someone must have dropped it. Somebody ate bread here. The small piece of bread dissolves into almost invisible particles when someone walks over it. Where does the bread come from? Who ate it? When did that person eat it? Was it in secret?

"We will not eat the rooster today!" [8]

DANCE OF THE DAY.

"It is about inviting others to enter a space where selftransformation becomes possible.

The outcome of this pedagogy is not to increase knowledge and not to consolidate one's subjectivity, but to arrive at a condition where the moment that one's subjectivity dissolves is at once

---

8. Words at *Decisions at the Food-bank*.

where it becomes possible to establish new relationships to one's actuality."[9]

I participate. We practice a reporting score borrowed from Authentic Movement.[10] I am a witness and a mover. Then we sit and talk from our own perspective.

I feel a tension which I felt before Through Practicing. An enormous tension between 'therapy' and 'art practice.' How can I go beyond this tension? The word 'art therapy' is used several times by participants. I tend to perceive it as a tension between 'the self' and 'de-subjectivation.' Does imagining ('art practice') erase the 'self'? Therapy always has a relationship to self-actualization.

A *tension* sounds like *attention*.

NERVOUS SYSTEM.

Watching. Not participating. Breathing. *Joined* breathing instead of joined attention.

My body becomes space.

FOOD AND FIRE.

Can I localize the rooster? Togetherness without any goals.

REPORTING AND ESSAYING
ON PRACTICE.

"And as always with speech one is blind. To speak is not to see."[11]

9. Maarten Simons and Jan Masschelein, School, pedagogy and Foucault's undefined work of freedom. PDF file. April 23, 2020. http://www.materialifoucaultiani.org/images/06simonsmasschelein.pdf
10. *Authentic Movement* is an expressive improvisational movement practice that allows a group of participants a type of free association of the body.

I am listening to the reporting session and reading *Essaying on practice* simultaneously. At the end of each day we have a group reporting session in which we share how the witnessed practices affect us and make us think. *Essaying on practice* is Alex Artega's first trial of performing his practice of writing exploratory essays publicly.

We have a conversation about questioning the practice of sharing itself. Is verbalizing what we experienced the only way of sharing? Does this practice stem from our need to grasp things and make them explicit? Or does it stem from our need for feedback? Or, rather, from our need to 'know' (in terms of wanting to produce explicit knowledge about what we experienced)? Is it possible to trust only the nonverbal? How might we share our experiences in a non-verbal way? We could have conversations without words. Is it bearable to not know? Does poet John Keats' beautiful idea of 'negative capability' (the ability to tolerate the pain and confusion of not knowing) create a possibility for a different kind of knowledge and thus of pedagogy?

> "An essay is a carefully attempt to modify our mode of being in the present. It is a 'transforming test of oneself in the pay of truth', or an 'askesis, an exercise of the self in thought'." [12]

I decided to practice silence and listening. Did 'I' decide this, or did the practice move me toward it? Is it a practice to be present and silent?

---

11. Maarten Simons and Jan Masschelein, School, pedagogy and Foucault's undefined work of freedom. PDF file. April 29, 2020. http://www.materialifoucaultiani.org/images/06simonsmasschelein.pdf.

12. Maarten Simons and Jan Masschelein, School, pedagogy and Foucault's undefined work of freedom. 2019. http://www.materialifoucaultiani.org/images/06simonsmasschelein.pdf

Is silence pedagogy?
Can we teach the ungraspable?

A beautiful reporting practice unfolds.

It cuts into the space. An installation which is interestingly not mentioned in the flyers is supposed to invite visitors through a technological set-up consisting of a screen, a camera, and a projector. This invitation does not reach me until we speak about it during the reporting session, which concludes the day. We are sitting on the round carpet, where the day also started. We share our fantasies, observations, and silences, produced for us by one and the same place and in different moments. Co-habiting the space, it becomes a place which is bigger on the inside than it is on the outside. The space became charged, filled with events, stories, emotions, emptiness, meaninglessness, uselessness.

    We speak in a 'blind' way, not knowing, just following a path and finding out along the way. A space I thought I had missed out on unfolds and shows what was unseen for me. Cut-in and fold-out.

And so it went.
    The rooster stayed untouched.
    Will the rooster die to be eaten or will it die of old age?
    And would someone bury him in the latter case, or would he disintegrate unrecognized?
    The unspeakable leaves a space.

Would this space witness us?

Unrequested Services

Simone Basani

The experience of joining ... *Through Practices* has made me realize different things. One of the most important ones is that for a long time now (at least seven years), I have been creating a discourse about the conditions of existence of my own practice, and other similar ones—but only in my mind. Thanks to the invitation made by Heike and Alex, I want to take the time, and hopefully find the appropriate words, to write these thoughts down.

I want to write about the conditions of existence of a specific kind of art practice—one that seems to have neither a single name nor a 'family tree,' or not just one name but several mothers and fathers. The complex relationship these practices have with their own genealogy intrigues me. It seems to make the existence of these practices insecure on a material and symbolical level. Yet, it allows them to resist falling under a category of beings that can be easily governed by institutions. Still, I think that it is possible to tackle the complexity of the structural features that constitute these practices.

I believe there is at least one feature they all share: they place the development of *politics of attention* at the core of their mode of subjectivation. When I say politics of attention, I mean that they work on organising the conditions under which collective acts of looking, of paying attention, of caring for someone or something take place. This happens on different scales and timings, at different levels, and through different networks of relationships.

But how does paying attention become an art practice?

When Isabell Lorey writes against governmental precarization—one of the dimensions of the precarious she takes into consideration—her reflection touches on a concept I find relevant here: that of self-empowerment practices. This concept is an ambivalent one for Lorey, since it "can signify modes of self-government that represent a conformist self-development."[1] However, at the same time, she recognizes that these practices "can also break through, refuse, or escape from appeals to functional self-government."[2]

The self-government of precarious lives theorized by Lorey seems to be a very productive dimension of practicing, since it embraces the incalculable. It trains and constructs these lives as *dangerous others* that can move, think, and create, both within and outside of "the political and social community, as *abnormals* and *aliens*."[3] Among those aliens, there are artists. Among the artists, there are individuals or groups whose practices of attention *are* practices of empowerment. This empowerment action is not only directed, however, towards themselves, but rather towards an organised group of participants or collaborators, where one could challenge her/his own capacity of *autonomy* within a *collectivity*.[4]

In my view, these art practices, apparently nameless, can be called *services*. The term *services* describes both what they are and what they produce. The sense I want to stress draws upon two meanings of the Latin roots of this word, and in particular to two meanings of the verb *servire:* 1) to pay attention to something or someone; 2) to be used.

Here, I think of *services* as art practices of collective empowerment, and from now on I will use this term in this text with such a meaning. These services can be used to refuse or escape from appeals to a functional and obedient way of self-government. Through these practices, the artists decide what to pay attention to, consider how to do this together with other people, and explore which form of government the practices themselves can take.

1. Isabell Lorey, State of Insecurity: Government of the Precarious (New York NY: Verso, 2015).
2. Id.
3. Id.
4. Valeria Graziano, "Recreation at Stake," in A Live Gathering: Performance and Politics in Contemporary Europe. ed. A. Vujanovic (Berlin: b_books, 2019).

In my view, this is possible because of the way these art practices are born: i.e. in an unrequested manner. This is another feature they all share. Differently from domestic, cleaning, sex services and the like, they are born unpaid, uncommissioned, and unrequested by institutions, patrons, groups of private citizens or committees of any sort. The challenge for the artists who develop these services is to build sustainable strategies that enable them to live interconnected with others, and to partner with institutions.

I will frame my concept of services further. First, let me dive into the concrete process of conceiving of and starting an art service. I will use a procedure from my own practice:

"Many environments catch my attention. They strike me even if I strive not to let them do so, and they move me even if I do not want to cry. When that happens, I start paying attention to their inner mechanisms, and to the social and political norms that govern them. This is how I start producing an unrequested service: by observing the way people move, how and what they ask, how they touch each other (if they do at all). However, what captures my attention even more powerfully is noticing my own reactions to what happens around me.

As in a science experiment, I start using myself as a litmus paper: I try to focus on the way my whole body (including my brain) reacts to this environment. A given colour on a litmus paper corresponds to a specific desire or need in my body. I look then at the way my desires and needs are affected by this environment. In this way, I can consider these desires as site-specific. From these feeling, I learn something I did not know about myself previously. How do I manage to move across this space? How is my body feeling next to the ones who are with me? Is there something I wish to do here? Why? With whom? Is there perhaps something missing here? How do the norms that constitute this place function? Which subjectivities are barred from being here? Am I among them? How could we empower ourselves by constructing something together that previously didn't exist here?

Most of the time, I end up conceiving services that I and other people could use in such situations—services that are, in my view, necessary, but that seem too difficult to be created, as no institution is asking for and, therefore, supporting them. Nevertheless, I allow myself to imagine them, very seriously.

From here, if I decide to give time to this creation process, I engage myself in a conversation with all the different spectators I have inside me. These are the ones who witness the life of those environments I am in: the Wandering Writer, the Restless Reader, the Intuitive Producer, the Half-Asleep Learner, the Analyser of Social Dynamics, the Angry Activist, and a few others. There are figures of attention whose personalities I got to know over time. They help me formulate ideas that are efficient enough to be proposed to other people: ideas for a service, which at this point, still has to grow. The concept of a specific service needs to be shaped, yet asks to be acknowledged in its specific features: 1) the fact that it cannot exist without the collaboration of other people; 2) the fact that it activates (old and new) skills of all the people involved, produces an action of empowerment, local networks of contacts, and productive clashes between different subjectivities; 3) the fact that it has been conceived with care—organically—in relation to my cultural knowledge, my social and artistic expertise, and my desires.

After this, comes the negotiation phase. This is when I want to find a strategy to gather possible collaborators and co-authors around the ideas I had, present them to this group, or these groups, and see which kind of collective project might emerge. These are the first ideas, which propose a precise direction and, at the same time, stay open to the individual or collective propositions of the group. Sometimes, the concept of the service gets dismantled completely within the negotiation process by the collaborators and co-author. Sometimes the negotiation brings the service towards its visualization/realization; sometimes it vanishes."

My aim here is to give a report of a procedure that can be used to conceive of and start a service. It is one of the possible procedures that many art institutions do not wish to recognize, or do not know how to recognize. When they do, most of the time they end up exploiting its outcome, because they see its social potential but not its *prestige value,* as Andrea Fraser would say.[5] They absorb the project itself into their programs without supporting their authors' research, labour, and production work. Another option is to liquidate the project straight away, transferring its co-authors or participants, into their own generally non-stimulating educational activities.

Since these unrequested art services are recognizable as actions of individual and collective empowerment, they are usually compared to a wide range of activities, such as those organised by education departments in museums, social organisations, or networks of activists. However, this comparison causes confusion in the process of understanding these art practices, if not even a mortifying feeling in those artists who creates services. These artists cannot, and do not wish to fit the agendas of social organisations and educational departments, or of activist manifestos. The reason is that their practices do not marry one ideology in particular, and do not promise any specific result on a social or artistic level before starting their process.

5. Andrea Fraser, How to Provide an Artistic Service: An Introduction. Lecture, The Depot, Vienna, October 1994. http://adaweb.walkerart.org/~dn/a/enfra/afraser1.html [Accessed April 22 2020]

The procedures used by these services do not to simply repeat pre-existing formulas of social engagement or empowerment. To re-create, mix, and transform those formulas is a fundamental part of their artistic concern.

Conscious appropriation, and even imitation, can obviously exist as in any other art form, but unrequested services would never uncritically borrow a formula or a technique. This is precisely because the ongoing research on attention, participation, and empowerment strategies is what defines the conditions of their own existence.

As I stated in the beginning of this text, the first feature of unrequested services is situating politics of attentions at the core of their mode of subjectivation, which I can now say is also their meaning. For this reason, unrequested services care mainly about the (dramaturgy of) experience of their collaborators, participants, and audience. Social dynamics are to services artists what the brush is to the painter.

There needs to be a new vocabulary, and therefore further investigation, for describing these practices of attention. There is also a need to write down the invisible genealogy of an inconvenient, non-consanguineous family of practitioners—a story unheard for so long, whose characters, alive or dead, do not know each other in person, or seem unaware of possible current alliances. There needs to exist a trans-historical and trans-disciplinary strategy to make space for an ecology of practices that consciously produces services, as an artistic and political act.

Who are the members of this family, and what are their names? They are artists with very different, often hybrid, educational backgrounds. Only some of them are well known; most of them are little known.[6] I am currently wondering where the forgotten ones lie or breathe at this moment, and how to (re)connect with them. There needs to be a statement that would re-position, or position for the first time, the services they have created in the artistic sphere they belong to. There needs to be an efficient, performative utterance.

For instance, a series of public pleas to unknown, unheard, or forgotten artists who produce services.

Let me address one artist, for now. Other ones might follow if needed. But for now, this plea sounds something like: "...be back, be with us, find words and names for those practices which never ended / which are always necessary and never ended / which need to re-organise production and condition of complex environments, in order to exist / in order to produce specific social use value / which claim that very re-organisation as an artistic invention / work with us, when we hold on, work with our practices / through contexts that try to disavow them / and witness those services that are always recognized by all the people involved in their creation."

This plea is to Danilo Dolci.

Dolci was an educator, architect, sociologist, and poet. His name, however, is largely forgotten these days on the pages of Italian cultural research publications, not to mention in the press, on television and in collective memory. In my view, this happened because his political profile is very difficult to label. He was an *alien* who received a very strong Catholic education as a teenager and young man, and always expressed his background until he decided to focus on anarchist thinking. I want to position him here as an artist of *unrequested* services, simultaneously on a social, political, and artistic level.

> 6. In the first group, there would be names as Tania Bruguera, her Catedra Arte de Conducta and her platform Arte Util, Theaster Gates and his Dorchester Projects, Granby Four Streets and their collaboration with Assemble, Mierle Laderman Ukeles and her manifesto, Andrea Fraser and her Services project, Mammalian Diving Reflex and all their unrequested Engagement services. In the second one there would be names like: La Brigada Puerta de Tierra and their Aqui Vive Gente, Helena Producciones and their Festival de Perfomance de Cali, Christa Donner and her Cultural ReProducers, etc.

A very efficient example of his services is, for me, a project that he created in Partinico, Sicily, in collaboration with more than 150 citizens including farmers, fishermen, fisherwomen, factory workers, intellectuals, and a large group of unemployed people. On the 2nd of February 1956, the large group decided to do, under Dolci's coordination, what nobody expected from them: going to work without pay. It was their *strike in reverse* and was not intended to be a performance in public spaces, but rather a form of unauthorized work. Their task was to rebuild one of the old local *trazzera,* which are roads in Sicily that go through fields and are mainly used by herds. They did it for two main reasons: to reopen the old trazzera, which has been neglected by local councillors for a long time, and to bring public attention to the surrender of local institutions. Called by Dolci, a group of journalists, photographers and cameramen were there to witness this event and document if for the whole country.

When the first police commissioner arrived, Dolci and the unemployed citizens quoted Article 4 of the Italian Constitution, which (still today) enshrines the right to work.[7] This was not the first strike, that Dolci organized *as service*. Nor was it the first strike in reverse in Italian history. The strike in reverse practice had already existed at that moment for around ten years. It was a nonviolent practice, through which groups of unemployed people organized themselves to peacefully re-open public works that were not delivered or neglected by local authorities.[8] But this is the one that has been communicated in the most efficient way to the press in the whole history of strikes in reverse, and participated by a very mixed, yet tight-knit, group of citizens. Given the composition of the group of participants or collaborators, their awareness of their collective actions, and the aims of their performative action,

---

7. Danilo Dolci, *Processo all'Articolo 4*, Sellerio, 2011.
8. Roberto Baldoli, *Reconstructing Nonviolence: A New Theory and Practice for a Post-Secular Society,* Routledge, 2018.

this particular strike in reverse can be considered, in my view, as an artistic re-invention of a pre-existing collective political practice.

Let's go back to the moment when the citizens and Dolci, in front of the Commissioners, appeal to Article 4 of the Italian Constitution. The police charged at them. Dolci was arrested, along with fifty others, mostly day labourers. In the next days, this strike in reverse sparked various protests in Rome, Repetto, and Palermo. During his prison term, Dolci wrote one of his most appreciated texts, *Processo all'articolo 4,* which still refers to Partinico events. His trial quickly became *cause célèbre*. A large group of national and international intellectuals embraced his cause.[9]

Even though the widespread attention caused by his clever communication tactics played a fundamental role in the this particular strike, what I would like to stress here is Dolci's practice of both paying and asking for attention—of looking and of listening. He managed to research previous strikes in reverse, to understand their dramaturgy, to gather more than 150 people from different professional backgrounds, and to negotiate with them the tactics to be used for the strike.

There was no political party behind him when he decided to move from the north of Italy to Sicily, where he started to organise co-operatives run by landless peasants, with nobody asking explicitly to organise what would become one of the most famous strikes in Italian history. What lies behind this *sciopero* is his poetic wish to create, through the collaboration with other citizens, an efficient image of a collective complaint and, at the same time, an empowering occasion to, finally, work. He created room for understanding that collective imagination can be used to

---

9. Gerardo Litigio, Solidarietà illegale, Bibliomanie, Saggi e Studi, 48, December 2019. Readable online too: https://www.bibliomanie.it/?p=1024. [Accessed April 22 2020]

realize something that is commonly depicted as useless or impossible. Something that can brilliantly, poetically fail. By embodying its own ideas and desires, and not just being supported by them, this service created *a precedent, a matrix* for other disobedient alliances and actions to follow.

Recent words spoken by Italian philosopher Leonardo Caffo (that "art prolongues, and pierces, time") make me think that Dolci's *sciopero* is an art service also because it sets its own tim(e)ing.[10] It asked the rest of the society to pay attention to the *sciopero,* and to follow the socio-political score that has been written by a group of people nobody had time for before it.

To conclude, I translate a statement given by Danilo Dolci during an interview in 1975. I like to think of *strike* here as a synonym or a specification of the word *service:*

> "I think that a strike should always be a form of knowledge as well as a work of art, an invention. National strikes with millions of people get to be organized, without being able to affect, to capture the attention of people, similarly to movements run by small groups of people which, however, know how to invent with accuracy (inventare esattamente). It is a matter of precision: moral and technical precision…"[11]

---

10. Leonardo Caffo, Essere giovane, essay (in process), found in Cosmo Digitale online exhibition. https://www.castellodirivoli.org/leonardo-caffo [Accessed March 3 2020]
11. Giacinto Spagnoletti, Conversazioni con Danilo Dolci (Messina: Mesogea, 2013).

ESSAYING ON PRACTICE

Essaying on Practice is Alex Arteaga's first trial of performing his practice of writing exploratory essays publicly and with the sporadic participation of other writers. Exploratory essay writing is one practice of very slow aesthetic observation. It consists of a detailed and intimate observation of a concept—in this case "practice"—conditioned by the agencies of all the elements of writing—the writing technologies, the body's actions, the syntax, semantics and morphology of the text and the elements of layout. This time the observation will be conditioned as well by witnessing the performance of other practices.

Short description of Alex Arteaga's practice as it appeared in the
...Through Practices program.

On Practice.
An exploratory essay (fragments)

Alex Arteaga

(with contributions of Hazal Arda, Silke Gerinkx, Heike Langsdorf, Laura Oriol, Einat Tuchman)

Moving. Doing. First of all.
    Action—acting, in a sense of being active, performing actions. Performing, in a sense of realizing actions, doing actions, acting—and, maybe also in a sense of understanding it. It: the action, the acting, what is happening by acting, through acting. Understanding, in a sense of participating in the collective process of emergence of sense in a way that makes sense for me/us—the one/s who is/are understanding—moving, acting, doing.

Taking a position? Is this a necessary foundational moment for practicing? That is, do we need first to take a position—or to position ourselves—in order to practice, to begin to practice—to begin to practice a practice?

Touch. Con-nection. Considering a field of shared agencies, that is, considering all implied entities as endowed with agencies, touch as the friction that makes possible the actualization of these agencies, as the moment or maybe better the form of relation, or maybe even better—a certain specification or even quality of relation that triggers the actualization of agencies, or more precisely, another possible enabling condition for agencies to come to be action, to liberate them from the realm of the potential, of the possible-but-not-yet, to actualize them.

Let's go back to positioning. First, maybe, to take a position in the space—geo-graphical, geo-logical positioning: to become a sign on the earth, to obey or simply be part of the logic of the earth.

To 'occupy a position,' we could also say, implying that the position was already there, before we position ourselves, before we 'take' the position that was already there, preceding our action of positioning ourselves.

Observing ourselves while practicing: our acting body—our practicing body—as object of observation, as agent co-constituting perceptions, images of itself.

Observing, as a primary option, as noticing—without elaborating on any other intentional actions but perception. 'Only seeing'—dwelling in the 'realm of the naked eye.'

Touching ourselves as bodies while we—maybe also we as bodies—are touching other components of the practice—other participants, other practitioners, of any kind.

Con-template. To intensify the chosen field of observation—our temple, our *temenos:* our practices, our practicing—and probably doing it in any kind of perceptual modalities—with others—any kind of others.

Sensing. Becoming aware. Through the senses—through the skin, through this particular part of myself, which envelopes my-self, which outlines my-self both physically and in terms of my identity, I was tempted to say, but maybe better: in terms of my-selfness-for-myself.

Looking at me in a mirror I see my skin when I'm seeing myself. I cognize and recognize myself when I see my skin, the element of my body that puts it in touch with its not-body—with the exterior, with its exterior, we tend to say, accepting uncritically the existence of an interior in my body or even myself as something situated in an ostensible inside of my body (which would be, consequently, not me but my container, the material condition for the interiority I inhabit).

Sensing, thus, through the element that allows me to be in touch with my-self and with my-not-self—with the other, the others, the rest, the not-me, the not-my-self.

Sensing, thus, necessarily, in a careful way—as if knowing that the exposure that propitiates the touch is as necessary and desired as potentially dangerous— as if knowing that the skin is thin, that the shield, the recognizable layer of the container of this ostensible interiority in which I assume to be situated—or even to be—can be easily damaged and even destroyed.

Opening as a way of activating the skin, as a particular way of actualizing its potentialities of touch, of connectivity, of, maybe, changing the balance between separating and connecting, questioning, maybe its self-asserting function in favor of a potentially destabilizing one, in favor of becoming an enabling condition for temporary dissolution and furthermore, maybe, redefinition.

Communication. Generation of signs. For others. With others but mainly for others. With others because it is for others—maybe, in some cases, for others in order to be with other/s.

     Observing others—taking their signs for us. Willing to take their-signs-for-us. Not of taking them in—accepting, again, this possibility—but rather operating in the surfaces that enact and receive—even reflect—these signs.

     Positioning yourself—to generate signs, to receive them, to reflect them, to reject them.

     Bodies being mobilized by the power of signs—of the signs touching them, of the signs they form.

Negotiating distances, proximities—physical, emotional, conceptual; physically, emotionally, conceptually. A dense network of intentional acts as enabling conditions for distances and proximities, coincident moves, dissonant directions to emerge.

Sensing the dynamics that relate consent and dissent. Sensing the getting together, going the same way or moving apart. Sensing the subtle oscillations between these two poles—the maybes, the rathers, the nuances, the dubitative moves, the approaches, the not-yet-but possible signs, the temporary breaks, the pauses… as possible scenarios of a change of inflection.

Interstices. Cracks in the process.
But also: sudden turns, clear determinations. The introduction of maybe unexpected vivacity, of resolution, of strength.

And outside the sun and the wind. People chatting. Another sphere of activity. Different movements, different sights, different varieties of attention. Different velocities, different postures, different bodies—different ways of becoming body. And especially, different ways of attending to the environment, of co-generating the environment: in the outside it seems to be given. No attention is needed for it to exist. But here, inside, in the space of practice, it seems to be emerging continuously, as the indirect result of very intentional and fully aware actions.
Outside everything seems—from here, from the space of practices—to be clear, easy, simply happening. Here—outside of the fluent space of the quotidian—every single move seems to be heavy or, at least, significant.

To 'carry the attention' intermittently. To try to carry it, although it works only intermittently. To try again and again. Accepting its absence, its weakness.
The state of pretending to be conditioned is the moment of surrendering for the attention: It gives up its pre-existing content and creates the absence that would be filled up by the suggestion of another—another person, or another state of mind. It is pretending because the

inscriptions in the space or the words will never take over the ever-moving-perception, but it will lead to absence where the creation of experience can take place.

Elaboration—working out, working to the outside, although not necessarily producing (leading to the outside). Not necessarily developing either. Rather continuing to work with it. Like kneading it. Not yet giving form, maybe. Not yet informing. Rather processing it—keeping it in a process: in its process, in a shared process which implies it and the one who elaborates on it. Creating the conditions of possibility of its information. Making it soft, coherent— with itself and for the one who is elaborating on it.

A practice as a means and maybe a medium for elaboration. A systematized set of actions, actors, and agencies able to process and to keep it in process—able to conduct a transformation.

Elaborating through organizing previously generated material. Elaborating on this material—or maybe on its object of reference, if any—through organizing it, creating different distributions, 'arranging'—as I hear. Through establishing different relationships.

Relational transformation: transforming through (re-) defining relations. A process of resonances, I could say. Of dynamic resonances: resonances changing due to the relation stablished between potentially resonating bodies. Modulations through variations of the way and the position from which relationships are established.

Practicing, thus, as disclosing or discovering?
As achieving or providing access?

Achieving access? Or accessing achievement?

Are the latter two different moments or two aspects of the very same one? Is the achieved not always accessible right away?

And what about elaborating on achievements?

Well I think in a sense, practice is immediate achievement as it fulfills itself just by doing. Sometimes though, just doing isn't enough. This could be problematic, as without witnesses our practice is not seen and thus taken into account in an end product. But just doing could be enough, if you make this decision. But that's a hard decision, no?

Doing, witnessing, producing, being taken into account…

What about an immanent approach to practice, at least in a first phase? What about approaching practice, first, in relation to the sphere in which it takes place, not aiming therefore to transcend this sphere but rather to transform it and its components—the practitioner(s), the media and materials of practice, and the object(s) of practice? This is also a very basic possible decision. Also a hard one…

I live with the fantasy that if I treat my life as a practice and if I implement creative practices into the designing of my life, I will achieve a certain kind of peace and acceptance. Curiosity will govern my days. But the fantasy works with the 'achievement' desire and kills curiosity. I'm exaggerating a bit, but emotionally it feels this way.

Curiosity is a particular attention given to matter—to things such as events, thoughts, emotions, the material of life. It's an inquiring attention that is both eager and patient. It's an attention that desires to understand things but knows how to give time to understanding. It is also a will to listen, observe, search for meaning. It's a kind attention that is even loving, we could say. A healing attention, in fact.
     Curiosity provides bridges. Perhaps curiosity is the desire to learn.

Does desire aim to grasp, to control, to somehow possess, while curiosity allows for the creation of open-ended relationships—bridges that can be built from both sides without preconceived form?
     I like to see desire differently. For me, it is a force. Curiosity is a good—for desire to come through, express, realize. And, yes it enables open-endedness, which is an edge that is both enjoyable and uncomfortable. I mean, curiosity helps me transform my need to resolve problems as the only way to approach problems.

A network of coexisting attentions—awarenesses, maybe. A network of lines of intentionality, of attentiveness. A dynamic network. An active and re-active network. An emerging sensorimotor system, I could say, delimited exclusively by those who configure the system from the inside, by those that co-constitute, again, an interiority—the place of the practice, the environment of the practice, the environment as the emergence of the emerging system of practices.

Practicing: inserting signs into the environment, intervening, interfering through the generation of singularities in the environment emerging out of the practices—or maybe more precisely, strongly conditioned by them. Intervening, thus, in the own intervention. A texting textile. A weaving texture.

Practicing: producing, sharing, distributing, explaining constellations, configurations—of signs, sign-based artifacts. Presenting—allowing for presences to appear and to be transformed. And, perhaps, transforming the references of the produced signs through the transformation of the sign-based artifacts. A dynamic meshwork of transformations, enabling one another, constraining one another. Initiated, triggered, motivated by guided, framed attention—awareness, maybe—by coexistent trajectories of intentionalities.

Going back and forth. Again and again. Closing and opening. Observing, producing, manipulating, showing, providing specific conditions for observation, observing again.

Trying to make understandable—*nachvollziehbar:* possible-to-be-followed, viable in a collective or at least sufficiently shared way. Attending and finally affirming, making gestures that confirm the just emerged *Nachvollziehbarkeit*—"I follow (the path you are laying down)," "I am with you," "I am with it," "I am with you and with it, approaching it, treating it as you do." Apparently, at least. Enough, apparently. Now, for a while. We will see—but I see now.

The emergence of a common. Through practices. Through sharing practices. Through a commitment, a disposition, at least, a willingness to practice with.

Aiming at nothing—I would say. Goalless although framed. Maybe not leading anywhere. But allowing for further actions—sustaining the viability of our actions, potentially.

Time, here, always a kind of space of possibilities. Time-for, without any transcending goal—any goal that transcends neither the containing and enabling time nor the actions performed in and with it. Time and actions as mutually generating media, as interconnected fields of agency.

Practicing: interconnecting media, establishing relationships between the media that enable us to perform practices. Therefore, practicing as processes of media extension, of media transformation.

Expanding the field of attention. Is there always a component of training in a practice? Does each practice sustain itself through the training of the practitioner through practicing? Are there other self-sustaining components in a practice? Is it part of the function of the environment a practice enables to sustain the practice?

Does the goalless character of these practices open up fields of awareness that could never be generated as the achievement of a goal?

Are these practices based on a precise balance between knowing exactly what the practitioner is doing and not knowing at all what she is doing? And especially not what-for?

Daring to experience danger through following and breaking the rules.
        Interesting to see the dynamics of attraction.

Being drawn to a center of action; is it maybe linked to a mimetic reaction... capacity... desire?

Is the conduction of intentionality a structural issue in these kind of practices? Intentionality not as the tool but rather the conduct—as the negative form of what is really happening in epistemic terms—in terms of understanding, transforming, disclosing. As the relationship between sound and silence enabled by certain kinds of composition—sound as enabling a frame for silence.

An indirect non-teleological strategy. A kind of double indirectness: approaching the non-directed in an indirect way.
      The connection of two absences: of a goal and of an aim of approaching this goalessness without specific direction. Actions, or maybe more precisely instructions to act, as a kind of excuse? As a kind of necessary something to activate nothingness—a potentially fertile nothingness?

Observing these moments of sharing, I tend to ask myself if this still follows the logic of the practice. Is this (still) a practice?
      Do likes and dislikes belong to it or do they rather evaporate the potentialities of practices?

How can the voices break their logic without erasing one another's personal wish to exist through their individual expression of good and bad?

Can sharing without any practice-related structure kill the transformative power of a common practice?

Sharing as concluding in order to understand the restrictions of the multiplicity of perspectives. Can we conclude the words through the body, through movement, through action?

Do open-ended practices have to conclude?

The need to talk is like a declaration of my existence, being recognized by others, and receive confirmation of love. I guess.

Does love need confirmation?

We are so afraid.

DANCE OF THE DAY

Dance Of The Day is a score for groups to collectively make and execute an accumulative choreography. The situations occurring enhance how one contributes to 'something'—to a possible structure or organisation—that is not yet a given. It makes tangible how we are always already regulating a scene that is yet unruled. This practice explores the performative, or reality-producing, capacity of movement.

Short description of Heike Langsdorf's practice as it appeared in the ... *Through Practices* program.

Curious Things

Heike Langsdorf

APPARATUS[1]

With ... *Through Practices* we faced a very concrete situation: the co-organization of a symposium. Instead of lectures and verbal debate, this symposium brought together artistic investigations 'in,' or more precisely 'through,' practice. Showing our concerns by presenting our practices was a way of rethinking the nature of a symposium. In retrospect, it was not our goal to create an alternative. However, while we were looking for the most appropriate circumstances for what was at stake, we discovered another option that was slightly, but significantly, different from what a traditional academic apparatus normally suggests.

POOR BEGINNINGS

How to cultivate a sense for being in a constellation? How to intuit something, not necessarily *together,* but through sharing and presenting practices to each other? In the beginning, I experience only a 'poor' intuition for how to organize a space in which people present and share elements of their practices: presenting should not imply perfections or conclusiveness, and sharing should not mean permanently connecting, matching, or coupling. What is needed is a process of listening to what is there, present, in *"con-stellation"*—not on

---

1. An initial collection of personal concerns provided headers of paragraphs for my contribution to *Thinking Conditioning through Practice* (2017), the first book of the series *Choreography as Conditioning*. Since, I have been revisiting them to continue thinking-through-writing in this framework. While writing, the initial list of terms underwent slight changes over the last two years. While making this contribution, another two terms, THEATRE GOING and THE STUFF GOING ON, were absorbed by the others. Two new terms, CONTROL *and* THE DANCE OF THE DAY, appeared for a first time.

the wide firmament at night, but in a specific spatial situation. And I enjoy the etymological sense of the word "constellation", "shining together".

VAGUE ENOUGH

In order to be in constellation, one does not need to undergo the same (inner) process, but rather to recognize a mutual appetite for inhabiting a space by listening and understanding *through* the presence of the other. During the first of many gatherings leading to the symposium *...Through Practices,* I expressed my wish to gather artists and their practices at the closure of a research project.[2] I wanted to create an environment in which diverse practices take place in spatial and temporal proximity. In this context, the practices would need subtle adaptations in order to accommodate visitors. The goal of *...Through Practices* was to better understand whether some artistic practices can be perceived as forms of researching. My personal research practice contains two, 'vague enough,' elements that I found while working. Their ambiguity is what allows me to investigate them: *Distraction as Discipline* and *Discrete Guidance*. They relate to a curiosity unfolding 'on site.' For such a curiosity to unfold, a manifold of clues on how to be in a proposed space is needed. Through this plurality of signs, people can figure out on their own how to move within a given, but 'vague enough,' setting.

OUT OF AUTONOMOUS WILL

Following an invitation means sympathizing—at least partially—with what can be felt in it.

> 2. *Distraction as Discipline—an investigation in the function of attention and participation in performance art, art pedagogy and artist writing* / research at KASK school of arts Hogent (Langsdorf & Luyten 2016–2019).

The symposium ... *Through Practices* proposed to participate in protocols and scores, initially composed by artists for themselves, and now adapted so that they could be shared with others. A graphically designed timetable provided written descriptions of what the space invited, and, as hosts, we were available to offer guidance whenever people asked for more introduction or directions. Our schedule was made to make schedules re-scheduled, fur sure, but obviously only when people 'autonomously' felt that there was something in them for them. Autonomous will is indeed opportunistic— opportune to one's own preferences. This is not a pleasant discovery, but a challenge to continue asking how certain concerns can become relevant to others.

ENGAGING

Some people report: "It was hard to enter the space; I was not sure what would happen." Or: "I didn't dare to walk away." Or: "I felt dragged out of my comfort-zone, it didn't feel safe." This makes me think how difficult it is to understand the 'ethos' of a place or moment, and within it to find out how to be with, or respond to, it.[3] This again recalls #metoo, the global movement against mental and physical harassment, which brought a new collective insight: there is no safe space without all of us co-creating it 'in situ' and without a recipe. Where exactly is fear located? How is it provoked? How open and 'hosting' can a space be in order to quell everybody's fears? What exactly do we feel when we can't say "no," yet we also can't say "yes"? I suspect that, often, we might be more insecure of our

---

3. "The 'genius' of a people, characteristic spirit of a time and place," / "habitual character and disposition; moral character; habit, custom; an accustomed place," / in plural: "manners". https://www.etymonline.com/word/ethos#etymonline_v_11658. [Accessed March 4 2020]

own 'engagement' than of the other. Might investigating our feelings with more sense for differentiation help us to understand what makes us fear what?

CHOREOGRAPHY AS CONDITIONING

Potentially, any movement conditions the context within which it occurs. What happens in a group, when people condition each other through being present together? For me, being in a group is like being immersed in a fascinating book. With the necessary scoring—bringing the necessary distance for viewing—I can witness myself sitting where power relations are not omnipresent, but made. I can behave as a dot, a letter, a word, full sentence, or an entire paragraph. All of the above influence the text differently. Choreography (movement in space which is organized and executed by and/or for groups) conditions both participants and witnesses. Realizing any possible organization of movement, it creates the scenes and sceneries we live by. Situations we step into happen on different scales: in zones such as a theatre stage or football field which an individual can easily read, in messier and unclear places such as big institutions, or in very complex or even ungraspable spheres such as local or global politics. My capacity for reading complex scenes and understanding how my movements influence the bigger picture is far from advanced. Step by step I may develop it.

THE DANCE OF THE DAY

With *The Dance of the Day,* I am researching how a situation is made and shaped, in and as a group. How do we co-steer the courses of actions around us? Might steering sometimes include passively surrendering? What can I want within ever-changeable 'states of affairs'? How to acknowledge silence and 'not contributing' as a form of communication? Doing *The Dance of the Day* three days in a row for two hours is just enough time to discern what can be at stake in this proposal. A few sessions can only allow for some first questions, issues and problematics to emerge. I am now interested to work with this score for two weeks with a group that commits to two sessions of two hours per day, without talking before or after the practice. How will the score adapt to the group that works through it? What kind of customs or manners will we produce?

THE PERFORMATIVE

What makes a person, a space, a text, or a 'setting' performative is the fact that it demands our attention. Attention, therefore, is constitutive of a situation where performativity is at work. Such a setting is organized in a way that certain processes can be launched, run, pursued, and finished, while others can actually 'be with' or witness them. The disadvantage of such a process is that it is gone once it is over. The resonance of what has been performed is dependent on bodies and minds wanting to revisit, memorize, or reiterate what has been drawn out in their reception. Any past event—unlike a dead body, not physically present, but consisting of layers—can be the object of an autopsy. During and after the fact, we can come to see what the consistency of the activity or activation exactly was. Writing a text or presenting a research practice can be as performative as making a law, launching a product, or campaigning. One could say that people seeing processes unfold, and then investigating them during and after the fact, adopt a simultaneously performative and 'researching' attitude.

MOUNT TACKLE (2017 / Revisited 2019)

Together with about fifteen other performers—colleague-practitioners and students—I am preparing for the opening of *Mount Tackle (Revisited)*. Focussing on things that have to be done, I feel how my concentration is distracted. The closing event of ... *Through Practices,* happening right now, enters my mind. This gathering is led by dear colleagues. I cannot be part of it as I need to be here. *Mount Tackle* is all about the impossibility of attending everything that's going on. Its basic logic is the inevitable missing out among a myriad of events. It makes people shift between panning and zooming in, getting distracted and returning to what one was focussed on. A certain landscape is erased after I missed a little storm: what was a lit and transparent installation is now just masses of stuff, horrifyingly changing place in the near to pitch dark. On the other side of the stage, people seem to enjoy a little soft concert in bright yellow light.

CONTROL

I lie on stage under a heap-like construction from wood and diverse plastic sheets. We are checking a cue for a moment that will happen ten minutes from now. The public will enter and, with them, all that we prepared will dissolve into a shared and uncertain space. In that sense, we prepare for a logic of togetherness opposing the momentary spatial conditions: now everything has its exact time and space. Soon, we will trigger the initial scene to show some first changes. This will launch subsequent processes, necessary for the desired space to unfold: one that paradoxically needs a kind of wild, uncontrollable response from the public. Now we are a chrystalized space; soon, we will decompose. There will be a couple of events in fixed spots at precise times, and a lot of space between those anchor points. We are following a score, with two minutes to go. The space is in control of us. The space is dependent on us: on the temporal structure and event-ness that we—performers and audience surrounded by an abundance of 'stuff,' Mount Tackle's accessories and scenography, and our mental processes—are providing for each other. We, the space and us, are truly entangled.

THE POWER OF DIFFERING FEELINGS

Everything is prepared; we have triple-checked our cues. I hear the doors open, people entering the space, voices, words. I feel their different ways of giving attention (or not), to the space we are in. I see shoes passing, mirrored in the black plastic covering the wooden floor of the theatre. I am lying hidden on the floor and I feel the vibrations caused by the many steps being taken. How much time has passed—twenty minutes? I feel a hand 'stepping' on mine, my cue to appear. About two hours later, in the bar of the theatre, some people ask me: "How was it tonight"? I remember many exact moments and how they felt. I don't have distance to actually synthesize what happened, though. I have trouble grasping one overall impression. I don't want to lose the pleasure of differentiating moments. Out of a fear to reduce an experience of multiple realizations—'the power of differing feelings'—I resist packaging what happened on stage into one memory.

TEMPORARY SOCIETY

I listen to a recording, dating from October 30, 2019: People are engaging in the reporting practice session of the last day of the symposium ... *Through Practices*. Points of view get clarified and (unconsciously or not) thoughts play together. Temporarily, utterances influence each other and values that emerge through them seem to mingle. After listening to the full recording, two interlinked issues resonate: the use of language and the yearning for connection. Things mentioned present various realities, often not attuned, but sometimes astonishingly related to one another, either utterly out of match or completely in sync. There seemed to occur awkwardness when someone felt that someone else resonated differently with one and the same thing.

Eventually, the conversation ends with acknowledging that things can be of different value to different people. From what I hear, I feel a struggle: it seems difficult to just stand with a 'finding' alone, uncommented by oneself or unconfirmed by others.

ATTENTION AND PARTICIPATION

A house in heavy reparation, a person aggressed in the streets, financial problems, winning a prize, a sick mother, the first child, allergies, addictions, yoga retreats, loosing or finding a partner, or becoming an activist: such (and other) things may consume a person completely, draw their attention towards a single point, create existential stress—positive or negative—or scatter the mind. The temporalities of a research environment are often seen as being in stark contrast with a world that urges and explodes. Exploring, questioning, and reconsidering can make us advance—they can 'update' what we know, as we continue with activities and actions that move us into possible futures. Having enough time to investigate 'through our practices' is a necessary joy that makes us consciously attend to, and participate in, our lives. How can we consider this a human right, rather than a privilege? May we—may I—stay curious...

APE#188

...*Through Practices*
Alex Arteaga and
Heike Langsdorf (eds.)

© 2021 Art Paper Editions
& editors (Alex Arteaga,
Heike Langsdorf)
© 2021 of the texts:
the contributors
All rights reserved,
including the right of
reproduction in whole
or in part in any form.

ISBN 9789493146723
www.artpapereditions.org
First edition of 500 copies

...*Through Practices*
is the fifth book of the
series *Choreography as
Conditioning*.

Series concept
Alex Arteaga
Heike Langsdorf

Contributors
Bilal Kamilla Arnout
Alex Arteaga
Simone Basani
Julien Bruneau
Anne Dekerk
Klaas Devos
Emilie Gallier
Laetitia Gendre
Miriam Rohde
Heike Langsdorf
Anouk Llaurens
Irene Lehman
Lilia Mestre
Fransien van der Putt

Editors
Alex Arteaga
Heike Langsdorf

Copy Editor
Tawny Andersen

Graphic design
6'56"

Printed and bound
in Tallinn.

Choreography as Conditioning is produced in the framework of the research project *Distraction as Discipline —an investigation into the function of attention and participation in performance art and art pedagogy* conducted by Heike Langsdorf in association with Anna Luyten at KASK / School of Arts, University College Ghent. The research project is financed by the Arts Research Fund of Diversity College Ghent.

Choreography as Conditioning 5 is coproduced by radical_hope, a platform for artistic research and co-creation.

All rights reserved. No part of this publication may be reproduced or transmitted in any form or by any means, electronic or mechanical, including photocopy, recording or any other information storage or retrieval system, without prior permission in writing from the publisher and the editors.

The feather one could find included in this book when first opening it is related to Bilal Kamilla Arnout's practice (page 73). No animal has been harmed.